# ADOLESCENCE AND CULTURE

**PSYCHOANALYSIS AND CULTURE**
Arnold M. Cooper, M.D. and Steven Marcus, Editors

**PSYCHOANALYSIS AND CULTURE**
**Arnold M. Cooper, M.D., and Steven Marcus, Editors**

John E. Mack, M.D.: Nightmares and Human Conflict

Peter L. Rudnytsky: Freud and Oedipus

Ellen Handler Spitz: Image and Insight: Essays in
Psychoanalysis and the Arts

# Adolescence and Culture

## AARON H. ESMAN, M.D.

COLUMBIA UNIVERSITY PRESS NEW YORK

COLUMBIA UNIVERSITY PRESS
New York   Oxford
Copyright © 1990 Columbia University Press
All rights reserved

LIBRARY OF CONGRESS CATALOGING-IN-PUBLICATION DATA

Esman, Aaron H.
Adolescence and culture / Aaron H. Esman.
p.   cm.—(Psychoanalysis and culture)
Includes bibliographical references and index.
ISBN 0-231-06972-3
1. Adolescence.
2. Culture.
3. Psychoanalysis and culture.
I. Title.  II. Series.
HQ796.E695   1990
305.23'5—dc20
90-2042
CIP

Casebound editions of Columbia University Press books are Smyth-sewn
and printed on permanent and durable acid-free paper

Printed in the United States of America

c  10 9 8 7 6 5 4 3 2 1

Book design by Audrey Smith

# CONTENTS

[ v ]

# ACKNOWLEDGMENTS

This work found its origin in a suggestion from one of the editors of this series, Dr. Arnold Cooper. I am grateful to him for providing me with the stimulus to organize and develop some long-standing but inchoate ideas. Thanks need also to be expressed to the Department of Psychiatry of Cornell University Medical College and its chairman, Dr. Robert Michels, for the grant of sabbatical leave that permitted me the luxury of time and place that made the work possible.

As the reader will note, some of the content refers to events and situations in Great Britain. To the staff of the British Library and to Ms. Jill Duncan, executive secretary and librarian of the British Psychoanalytic Institute, I owe untold thanks for their helpfulness and patience in providing me with research material. The staff of the Payne Whitney Clinic Library and the Samuel J. Wood Library of the Cornell University Medical College have also been of great service to me. Ms. Marie Green has labored devotedly at typing the various drafts of the manuscript.

Throughout I have, as always, enjoyed the encouragement and support of my family and, in particular, of my wife, Rosa, whose critical comments have improved the text. To her I affectionately dedicate this volume.

# ADOLESCENCE AND CULTURE

# 1

# Adolescence
# in History

Probably the outstanding fact about contemporary adolescents is their visibility. Never before in history have young people, at least in the industrialized world, been so blatantly *present* in their modes of dress, their hairstyles, their musical tastes. As communication becomes faster, transportation easier and cheaper, and the spread of new ideas and new fashions from one center to another ever more rapid, it becomes more and more difficult for the observer to distinguish indigenous national trends. The Cologne punker more and more resembles the London original; Moscow rock apes, more or less successfully, its New York model; the Paris-designed miniskirt shows off the slender legs of the Japanese girl who wears it on the Via Veneto.

How are we to understand this apparent evolution of a global adolescent culture? Does it reflect universal biopsychological needs? Is it the consequence of media influences? To what degree are socioeconomic forces at play here, in contrast to intrinsic developmental pressures? This book will attempt to address such questions, as it explores the interpenetration of adolescence and culture—adolescence as a phase of individual development, culture as the matrix within which such development occurs and from whose impact it is inseparable.

Classical psychoanalytic theory has emphasized the central role of biological factors in the adolescent process; puberty—the maturation of the sexual apparatus and its consequent impact on drive/fantasy formation—has been viewed as the critical determinant of changing patterns of object-relations and behavioral trends (Freud 1905; A. Freud 1958; Blos 1962). Adolescence has been described as the "adaptation to puberty." Social science has emphasized, on the other hand, the determining influence of changing social role expectations in the transition from child to adult status in society (GAP 1968; Csikzentmihalyi and Lanson 1984). In his seminal work, *Childhood and Society*, Erikson (1950) sought to integrate these perspectives, creating a psychosocial model that emphasizes the consolidation of a sense of "identity" as the nuclear developmental issue of adolescence in any cultural setting.

All of these viewpoints—psychoanalytic, social science, "psychosocial"—take as their starting point the notion that adolescence is, in fact, a defined and definable phase of human development. It would be useful, however, to review this assumption in a historical perspective. Has adolescence always and everywhere been so recognized? When did our present conception of adolescence emerge? How does it compare with those current in earlier eras and in other types of societies? Of the state of affairs in classical Greece we know less than we should like, and the evidence is conflicting. In Sparta (Andrews 1967) young males were organized for military training from 14 to 20; they were separated from their families and subjected to rigorous physical regimens, which included whipping ceremonies and other ordeals. This certainly did not represent a "moratorium" in Erikson's sense; although young males were thus defined as a transitional social group, its characteristics did not correspond to our conception of adolescence as a period of experimentation in the pursuit of independence and self-determination. For the Spartan youth, "identity" was foreclosed; he was destined to become a soldier in the army of a military despotism.

In Athens, where military training was less rigorous and less protracted, taking place only from 18 to 20, the "ephebe"* occupied a recognized place in the social structure, at least of the upper social classes. (We know little about the lower orders in classical Greece.) In the fifth century B.C. and earlier, military training was obligatory and was the main defining activity of the ephebe; from the fourth century B.C. onward (thus in the time of Plato and Aristotle) it was voluntary, and many of the epheboi chose the more pacific education of the Academy where, as Plato tells us, they participated along with adults and perhaps some younger adolescents in the learned discussions. As

* The term *ephebe* means "one who has passed puberty," but no true age grade appears to have existed for those under 18.

such they were not sharply defined in the educational system. Aristotle described the gilded youth of his time in strikingly modern terms:

> The young are in character prone to desire and ready to carry any desire they may have formed into action. Of bodily desires it is the sexual to which they are most disposed to give way, and in regard to sexual desire they exercise no self-restraint. They are changeful, too, and fickle in their desires, which are as transitory as they are vehement; for their wishes are keen without being permanent, like a sick man's fits of hunger and thirst. They are passionate, irascible, and apt to be carried away by their impulses. They are the slaves, too, of their passion, as their ambition prevents their ever brooking a slight and renders them indignant at the mere idea of enduring an injury; for superiority is the object of youthful desire, and victory is a species of superiority. . . .
> Their lives are lived principally in hope, as hope is of the future and memory of the past; and while the future of youth is long, its past is short; for on the first day of life it is impossible to remember anything, but all things must be matters of hope. For the same they are easily deceived, as being quick to hope. They are inclined to be valorous, for they are full of passion, which excludes fear, and of hope, which inspires confidence, as anger is incompatible with fear, and the hope of something good is itself a source of confidence. . . . Youth is the age when people are most devoted to their friends or relations or companions, as they are then extremely fond of social intercourse and have not yet learned to judge their friends, or indeed anything else, by the rule of expediency. If the young commit a fault, it is always on the side of excess and exaggeration; for they carry everything too far, whether it be their love or hatred or anything else. They regard

themselves as omniscient and are positive in their assertions; this is, in fact, the reason of their carrying everything too far. Also their offenses take the line of insolence and not of meanness. They are compassionate from supposing all people to be virtuous, or at least better than they really are; for as they estimate their neighbors by their own guilelessness, they regard the evils which befall them as undeserved. Finally, they are fond of laughter and consequently facetious, facetiousness being disciplined insolence. (Hall 1904)

Best known, of course, is the pattern of sexual development of such upper class adolescent males. Between 14–16 and 18–20 they entered into homosexual relationships with older males (20 to 30), playing the passive role in what appears to have been primarily intercrural intercourse. When at 20 they emerged from their military training they would then assume the active role in such relationships, ultimately marrying at about 30 and becoming exclusively and, if we are to judge from Aristophanes, militantly heterosexual (Lacey 1968). Girls appear to have married early (typically at 14) in order to preserve their virginity for their husbands; for them, at least, adolescence and puberty appear to have coincided.

From this description it would appear that at least among the affluent upper classes of late Hellenic and Hellenistic Greece, a defined category of youth, if not an actual "adolescent" class, was recognized. However this may have been, it seems that with the decline and fall of classical civilization and the onset of the Middle Ages the definition was lost. Such, in any case, is the view of the French cultural historian Philippe Aries (1962), who maintained that, at least in Western Europe, "until the 18th century adolescence was confused with childhood." "In Latin the word 'puer' and the word 'adolescens' were used indiscriminately . . . a boy of 15 is referred to as 'bonus puer' while his younger schoolmate of 13 is called 'optimus adolescens' " (1962:35). *Enfant* was the universal French word for all preadults, e.g., a sexually promiscuous 15-year-old was referred to as an "enfant." Similarly, Aries pointed out, the schools, until the seventeenth century, did not distinguish between the child and the adult. Although the establishment of the Academy as a transitional institution between the school and adult life represented a beginning recognition of an intermediate stage, corporal punishment was meted out in the schools indiscriminately to children and adolescents alike; this measure minimized the distinction between these age grades while emphasizing that between childhood and adulthood.

In the sixteenth and seventeenth centuries, Aries noted, children from 10 to 13 sat in the same classes with adolescents of 15 to 20: "People went to school when they could, early or late" (ibid.:330). This situation is reminiscent of the rural American one-room schoolhouse, in which age levels were merged and which children attended when and as their duties on the farm permitted.

It was only in the eighteenth century, Aries stated, that a "new sensibility" emerged, marked by the appearance of two cultural prototypes, the "Cherubin" and the "conscript" —the former, as delineated by Beaumarchais and immortalized by Mozart, a love-struck, dandyish, pre-Romantic courtier; the latter, the young soldier, more virile, emphasizing hardiness and bravery. Figaro's aria "Non piu andrai" details the contrasts between these types, as he twits Cherubino on his impending enforced transition from the former to the latter. These newly constituted models of *jeunesse* represented "a new concept . . . in embryonic form . . . the concept of adolescence" (Aries 1962:268).

Most contemporary students have accepted Aries' magisterial authority. Sebald concurs that "prior to and throughout the Middle Ages children passed directly into the adult world between ages 5 and 7" (1984:10), and notes that "teenagers of the Middle Ages sometimes made history at an age when modern teens are still going to high school" (ibid.:12), e.g., Jeanne D'Arc. Although he cites Macaulay's references to youthful gang behavior in seventeenth-century London, he maintains that it was only with the industrial revolution that the requirement for more extended formal education led to the defining and institutionalization of a period between childhood and adulthood.

Kaplan (1984) designated Jean-Jacques Rousseau as, if not the "inventor" of adolescence, the first to identify and codify it. His *Emile*, published in 1762, around the time cited as critical by Aries, proposed a system of education, centering on the 15–20-year age span, that exemplified his central moral and educational theories, including the necessity for the delay of sexual consummation pending the acquisition of the rudiments of ethical sensibility and virtue.

Questions do arise, however. Even Aries cites an ancient document, *Le Grand Proprietaire de toutes choses*, a sixteenth-century version of a thirteenth-century Latin compilation of Byzantine texts, which speaks of adolescence as lasting from age 14 to an ill-defined end point (21? 28?) and marked by sexual maturation and physical growth. Shakespeare deals with adolescents in varied ways; most familiar, perhaps, is the oft-quoted passage from *The Winter's Tale*: "I would there were no age between sixteen and three-and-twenty, or that youth would sleep out the rest, for there is nothing in the between but getting wenches with child, wronging the ancientry, stealing, fighting."

Even more telling, perhaps, is *Romeo and Juliet*, not merely a tale of star-crossed lovers, but one of street fighting between what we would now call adolescent gangs warring over turf and reacting with fatal violence to slights and challenges to their virility—readily transposable to the twentieth-century urban scene as in the Sondheim/Bernstein *West Side Story*. Even in *Hamlet*, the University of Wittenberg seems to have been a setting in which Rosenkrantz and Guildenstern, along with the ambiguously aged protagonist, enjoyed some period of a "psychosocial moratorium" before the sanguine events at Elsinore led the prince to his fatal "identity crisis."

Kris (1948) and others have pointed out that Shakespeare's account, in *Henry IV*, of the adventures of Prince Hal is a classic depiction of mid-to-late adolescent development in an Eriksonian framework—a *Bildungsroman avant le lettre*. At first, in his youthful carousings with Falstaff and his gang of thieves and highwaymen, Hal is experimenting with what Erikson called "negative identity" fragments through trial identifications with antisocial figures who, at least in the case of Falstaff himself, served as father surrogates as well. (It should be noted, however, that with his customary political sagacity, Shakespeare represents Hal as an observer, but never as a participant, in delinquent activities.) Hal even plays with an overt oedipal triumph with distinct patricidal overtones when he prematurely tries on his dying father's crown. But when Henry IV dies, Hal immediately takes on his destined adult identity as king; he dramatically, even cruelly, rejects Falstaff and, in doing so, casts off the negative identifications with which, in his irresponsible adolescent years, he could afford to toy. In short, he becomes Henry V. Thus, at least according to Shakespeare, in the circle of the royal court it was possible even in late-medieval England for something resembling a modern adolescence to be lived out—or at least imaginatively reconstructed. Time and the wealth with which to purchase it were the necessary conditions—then as now.

Aries' picture of the emerging conception of adolescence in Europe is complemented by Kett's (1977) comprehensive and scholarly review of the history of adolescence in the United States. Like Aries, Kett concludes that adolescence arrived late in American consciousness and that the adolescent as a personality type appeared on the scene even later. In the largely rural America of the seventeenth and eighteenth centuries one was a "child," a "youth," or "young person," perhaps, but at least after the age of 7 or 8 one mixed with adults in many settings, attended school at unfixed times with school fellows of varied ages, and often left home early to find work or enter apprenticeship. The 14–16-year-old was an economic asset, even an economic necessity, in the large families of the time and, except for a small elite group, did not enjoy the luxury of a "psychosocial moratorium."

It was, Kett pointed out, only in the nineteenth century, with increasing urbanization and industrialization, that regular school attendance became the rule up to age 14 and that specific institutions for youth, like the high school, the YMCA, and church youth groups, became established. It was with the codification of age grading in the schools and the spread of the high school as a setting for the education and retention of older teenagers that the term *adolescence* came into general currency in the midnineteenth century, a time when, as Kett notes, moralists were becoming concerned about the frailty of youth in the face of the "temptations" of urban life.

Meanwhile, significant changes were occurring in the structure of the family. Greater longevity, along with fewer children more closely spaced, led to the proliferation of families in which both parents lived to see their children pass, often simultaneously, through the teen years and to lavish parental concern upon them. At the same time, technological change was drying up vocational opportunities for those in the 12–14-year age group, with the consequence that the age of home leaving advanced progressively. "Today," says Kett, "parents look at middle age as a time when their teenage children will place an extraordinary drain on family resources. In nineteenth-century families the opposite was true: teenage children were economic assets and were expected to compensate by their earnings for the fact that they had been economic liabilities when young" (1977:169). Increasing perception of these years as problematic, as a crucial period in the shaping of the adult soul, culminated in Hall's formalization of the concept of the adolescent as, in Kett's words, "the very bud and promise of the race" (ibid.:217).


Preliterate non-Western cultures provide another window on the question of the origins of adolescence. As Gadpaille points out, there appears to be no culture that does not in some way recognize and deal institutionally with what he calls the "sexual component of puberty." "The entire style of a culture may come to bear on how it responds to adolescent sexuality," he says (1977:148). Most significant in this regard is the ubiquity of the mother-son incest taboo. Variously interpreted, it appears to be the universal bedrock of human culture. Thus, in the sense of the purely biological aspects of pubertal development, "some form of sexual adolescence . . . is innately imperative in any culture" (ibid.:149).

In many cultures, however, this "sexual adolescence" is associated with a major change in social status, and it is this social adolescence that is marked by a wide variety of "rites of passage" that serve to institutionalize the transition from child to adult role and its specific meaning in each society. Van Genepp (1908) pointed out that in the totemic societies of Australia the emphasis in these rites is on separation from the mother and symbolic rebirth into the world of men. (Note that the stress is on a transition in the locus of affiliation rather than on the attainment of "autonomy": the latter is a Western concept unknown to most preliterate societies.) In warrior tribes, such as the Plains Indians in the United States, whipping was commonly employed. Rationalized as a means of inculcating toughness, it clearly symbolized, as do such procedures as the knocking out of teeth, ritual genital mutilation, and the Eastern European Jewish mother's slap on the cheek of her newly menstruating daughter, the ambivalence and envy of the adult toward the pubertal child and the wish to assert or reinforce adult authority (see Muensterberger 1961).

In any event, to deviate from or to rebel against such rites of passage is, as Gottlieb, Reeves, and Ten Houten (1966) point out, unknown and unthinkable in such cultures; to do so would be to divorce oneself totally from the society, since there is no available role for those who might seek

[ 13 ]

such deviation. Where the initiation process involves the whole age grade it serves to reinforce group cohesion and acceptance of or submission to the prevailing values of the society. In this such peer groups differ from those that arise spontaneously in our culture and are frequently defined, at least in part, by their antagonism to "adult" values.

The process of transition from child to adult status in such societies is generally brief. For the most part children learn their occupational and social roles during late child-hood (what Freud called the "latency period") and the lim-ited technology of the culture is transmitted either by par-ents or by designated parent surrogates. The rites of passage may last from hours to days, less often weeks, rarely longer. Of course, Mead (1928) has described (and Gauguin painted) an idyllic neo-Paradise in which adolescents engaged in free, protracted, leisurely experimentation with sexuality in the midst of an Edenic abundance that required no active pur-suit of adult economic role patterns and imposed, therefore, no rites of passage. Mead's depiction of the process of "com-ing of age in Samoa" has, however, been sharply challenged (Freeman 1983); it has been suggested that she, like Gau-guin, was engaged in a process of mythopoiesis, setting up an idealized alternative to the conflict-laden, repression-ridden youthful sexuality that, at least as Mead and Gauguin saw it, characterized the Western culture of their times.

For Mead a principal source of that view was Freud. Al-though most explicitly spelled out in *Civilization and Its Discontents* (1930), this theme, "the irremediable antago-nism between the demands of instinct and the restrictions of civilization may be tracked," says Strachey in his Intro-duction, "back to some of Freud's earliest writings" (60). As

Strachey points out, in one of the early letters to Fliess Freud observed that "incest is antisocial and civilization consists in a progressive renunciation of it" (Freud 1950); further, in the *Three Essays* he spoke of "the inverse relation holding between civilization and the free development of sexuality" (Freud 1905:242). "Respect for this barrier," said Freud, "is essentially a cultural demand made by society; society must defend itself against the danger that the interest which it needs for the establishment of higher social units might be swallowed up by the family, and for this reason, in the case of every individual, *but in particular of adolescent boys,* it seeks by all possible means to loosen this connection with their family" (ibid.:225; italics added). It was against the background of this picture of adolescent sexuality in civilized society that Mead reported—or created—her picture of the unfettered and guilt-free sexuality of Samoan youth.

Rites of passage may, as a culture changes in response to new conditions, take on new meanings as they lose their original significance. A case in point is the Jewish rite of bar mitzvah, which in its historically obscure origin marked the pubertal transition of the boy from child to adult status in the Jewish community, including the assumption of familial and economic as well as religious responsibilities.

The gain for the boy was substantial—the right to participate, along with adult men, in learned discussions of the Law and its interpretation: to play a part, that is, in the central concern of Jewish cultural life. The bar mitzvah persists in our time as a formalized rite of passage (Arlow

1951), but except in the most orthodox subcultures its meaning has become not only attenuated but transformed. The passage at 13 into "adult" status in nonorthodox or secularized middle class Jewish society is essentially meaningless, since neither psychosexually nor economically is the boy prepared to participate in adult life. And in most cases his bar mitzvah represents the end, rather than the beginning, of his involvement in the religious community. The bar mitzvah thus has become largely an occasion for social display and conspicuous consumption—a kind of middle class potlatch. Lavish gift giving (fountain pens, watches, stock shares) maintains in vestigial form some of the original symbolism. It is primarily among the hasidim, who have most vigorously resisted the incursions of modernism, that the original significance persists (Shaffir 1974).

What, then, are we to conclude about adolescence as a developmental phase? The bulk of evidence supports the view that adolescence, as we know it, is a "cultural invention" (Stone and Church 1957)—a product of industrialization, of the need to extend the period of education and training for adult roles in the face of expanding technology, and of the need (to be detailed in a later chapter) to keep young people out of the labor force in order to assure job opportunities for adults in times of scarcity. The "moratorium of choice" of which Erikson speaks is conceivable only in a culture in which choices are available; for the child in a preliterate or traditional culture the choice is to follow one's predestined way or to leave the society altogether.*

* There are those rare individuals who find in the vocation of the shaman an alternative role. Even this is, however, institutionalized in the culture.

Puberty has, of course, always been with us, and some process of adaptation to it, of assimilation into the body image of the newly acquired sexual capacities and the concurrent growth spurt, is certainly universal. Similarly, some process of socialization, of direction and channeling of sexual impulse, of inculcation of cultural values, is an essential component of all human societies. But the form with which we are familiar—protracted, indeterminate, conflict-laden, marked by gross dyssynchrony between sexual and social maturity—is our own cultural property and is by no means intrinsic to human biological nature or necessary for adaptation across the broad span of human social organization. In the words of Heinz Werner, ". . . in primitive societies there is an abrupt break between the two rigid social patterns of childhood and manhood, a break clearly defined by the initiation ceremonies. In advanced cultures there is a slow, long-lasting plastic transformation from one stage of life into the other" (1948:27).

# 2

# Adolescence as a Developmental Phase

In 1904 G. Stanley Hall, professor of psychology at Clark University, where five years later Freud was to make his momentous debut on American soil, published a two-volume tome under the imposing title of *Adolescence and Its Relation to Psychology, Anthropology, Sociology, Sex, Crime, Religion, and Education*. Hall's encyclopedic study became the established source for conceptualization and description of adolescent behavior for generations to come. In particular, Hall's model of adolescent "Sturm und Drang," based in large measure on European Romantic fiction as typified by Goethe's *Sorrows of*

*Young Werther,* became the prototype for later psychiatric and psychoanalytic representations of pubertal and postpubertal development. Hall spoke of the adolescent's "alternation between inertia and excitement, pleasure and pain, self-confidence and humility, selfishness and altruism, society and solitude, sensitiveness and dullness, knowing and doing, conservatism and iconoclasm, sense and intellect" (1904:40). The normal adolescent was conceived of as tempest-tossed, torn by unmanageable passions, impulsive, rebellious, and given to florid swings of mood. His relations with parents and the adult world in general were seen as antagonistic and conflict-ridden—a pattern later to be designated as "the generation gap." As Friedenberg later put it, "adolescence *is* conflict—protracted conflict—between the individual and society" (1959:32).

This picture of "normal adolescent turmoil" was epitomized, a half century later, by Anna Freud, who in a series of papers (1958, 1969) spoke of adolescence as a "developmental disturbance" and declared that it was frequently impossible to distinguish aspects of normal adolescent behavior from severe psychopathology of the neurotic, borderline, or even psychotic type. "I take it," said she, "that it is normal for an adolescent to behave for a considerable length of time in an inconsistent and unpredictable manner; to fight his impulses and to accept them; to ward them off successfully and to be overrun by them; to love his parents and to hate them; to revolt against them and to be dependent on them; to be deeply ashamed to acknowledge his mother before others and, unexpectedly, to desire heart to heart talks with her; to thrive on imitation of and identification with others while searching unceasingly for his own identity; to be more idealistic, artistic, generous, and unselfish than he will ever be again, and also the opposite: self-centered, egoistic, calculating" (1958:275).

Similarly, Friend contended that "the normal developmental crisis aspect of adolescence often makes it difficult to distinguish between health and disturbance" (Solnit 1959:523). Geleerd proposed that "partial regression to the undifferentiated phase of object relations is an essential factor in normal ego development in adolescence" (ibid.:530). "Rapid shifts" in identification and in loyalties and interests and rebellious behavior were posited as characteristic of the pattern of normal adolescence. These mercurial changes were understood primarily as defensive responses to the reactivation, under the influence of libidinal drive pressure, of unresolved oedipal conflicts, made more dangerous by the adolescent's newfound capacity for sexual consummation.

The force of Hall's authority and the predominance of clinical experience as the source of data for the psychoanalyst determined the dominance of this viewpoint for several decades. It was not until the 1960s that reports began to emerge of systematic studies of normative populations of adolescents. Studies such as those of Douvan and Adelson (1966), Symonds and Jensen (1961), Offer (1969), and Offer and Offer (1975) cast new light on the process of normal adolescent development. Although these studies were, of necessity, limited to a phenomenological perspective and to reports of conscious experience, Offer argues that, for his research at least, the development of an "alliance" with their subjects and the use of psychoanalytic perspectives in "listening" for the material of their interviews permitted the formulation of hypotheses about unconscious phenomena as well.

The thrust of most, if not all, of the normative population studies has been that, as Oldham (1978) put it, normal adolescent turmoil is a "myth." The researches of Offer and his associates, based on the work of over two decades, are probably the most extensive and certainly the most psychoanalytically informed of these investigations. These workers found that there were in essence three patterns of male adolescent development, to which they referred respectively as "continuous," "surgent," and "tumultuous." The continuous developers, who represented 23 percent of their largely middle class sample, showed a pattern of smooth, unruffled progression throughout adolescence and into young manhood. Their backgrounds were characterized by healthy and intact families, by parental support of their growing independence, and by a lifelong pattern of stable supportive peer relations. They were generally satisfied with themselves and with their place in life and were, in essence, models of mental health. None of the members of this group had shown any clinical psychiatric illness.

The second or surgent group, which comprised 35 percent of the total sample, was characterized by a generally sound pattern of adaptation, but with somewhat more emotional conflict, with periods of some progression and regression, with a certain amount of turmoil in the early adolescent period, and with some self-questioning, sexual anxiety, and mild emotional constriction. By and large, however, their development was characterized by adequate adaptation and general developmental success, though as might be expected, there was somewhat more conflict with parents in this group than in the "continuous" group. Some 36 percent of the clinical syndromes manifested in the total population came from this surgent segment.

The third pattern was that of "tumultuous growth." These adolescents made up 21 percent of the total study population and appear closest to the classical pattern of adolescent turmoil. Many of them showed overt behavior problems, intergenerational conflict, wide mood swings, and so on. Not surprisingly, about half of the clinical cases came from this group. A fourth group comprising about 21 percent of the total study population showed a mixed pattern, with features of two or more of these subgroups that made it difficult to classify them. Overall, however, at least two-thirds of the total group developed in a manner inconsistent with the classical picture of "adolescent turmoil."

Similar reappraisal of female adolescent development has been under way in recent years, inspired in considerable measure by the women's movement. Although systematic studies of normal female populations are few, stereotypes regarding both development and behavior pattern have been challenged and modified in response to broad scale reappraisals of female psychology. Traditionally the young girl was, like her male peer, thought to follow a stormy and troubled course through her adolescent years. In particular the conflict between her new strivings for autonomy and her powerful dependent longings for her mother were thought to lead defensively to a phase of "pseudoheterosexuality" in preadolescence and early adolescence (Blos 1961), along with an intense surge of bodily preoccupation related to pubertal changes and the feelings associated with them. This narcissistic concern was said to occur at the expense of true object relations, particularly with parents, from whom a protective distance had to be assumed to ward off both oedipal urges and preoedipal dependent wishes.

Barglow and Schaefer point out, however, that this "classical description is untrue to the facts of normal experience and is based on an archaic closed-system model of psychic energy distribution." The normal 13 to 15-year-old girl "can," they say, "relate with full affective intensity to parental objects and peers." Further, they maintain, adolescent " 'narcissism' . . . affords the yet emotionally vulnerable and regression-prone adolescent girl . . . valuable phase-appropriate protection" (1979:206) against premature and prematurely intense heterosexual experience. And along with others they challenge traditional notions that "passivity" and "masochism" characterize the fantasies that accompany early adolescent crushes—and, indeed, female sexual wishes in general.

"In conclusion", they assert, "normal [female] development may be less dangerous, frightening and 'volcanic' than the predominant portion of past analytic writing about adolescence indicates" (ibid.:209). Their conclusions concur, thus, with those of Offer and his associates, whose data have come primarily from the study of adolescent males. Kirkpatrick further maintains that the oft described "dropping off of academic performance in adolescent girls, the fear that 'success' will compromise femininity . . . is a *pathological* inhibition of aggression in the service of social restraint . . . it is not mature femininity" (1989:20, my italics).

As noted earlier, it has been a staple of the psychiatric and psychoanalytic clinical approach that normal adolescents manifest behaviors that are difficult if not impossible to distinguish from forms of severe psychopathology and that therefore clinical assessment of mental illness at this stage of development is hazardous and fraught with difficulty. A corollary thesis, beloved of the family doctor and others, was the notion that whatever deviant behavior the adolescent showed, it was just "growing pains" and he would "grow out of it."

A sizable nail was driven into the coffin of this point of view by Masterson (1967, 1968), whose long-term follow-up study of patients treated at the Payne Whitney Clinic showed conclusively that these disturbed adolescents did not "grow out of it." In brief, Masterson found that of the adolescents studied who showed clinically significant behaviors, the great majority continued to manifest clinical syndromes after a five-year follow-up period. For the most part their behavior patterns became consolidated into well-defined clinical diagnoses, and few if any of them showed substantial remission in their clinical disorders. As a result Masterson drew the conclusion that adolescent pathology was a very different thing from normal adolescent development and that the burden of proof lay on any clinician who chose to assess tumultuous or disorganized development in adolescence as "normal adolescent turmoil." Strober, Carlson, and Green (1981) have recently reported similar findings regarding the reliability of DSM-III diagnoses of adolescent patients.

## "Generation Gap"

Another staple of the popular literature on adolescence and youth, particularly in the 1960s and 1970s, was the concept of the "generation gap"—an ostensibly unbridgeable chasm between the values, attitudes, tastes, interests, styles, and behavior of young persons and those of their parents, between the rising generation and those already in authority or decline. In her discussion of the distinction between traditional ("post-figurative") and Westernized ("co-figurative") societies, Mead defines the latter as ones "in which the prevailing model for members of the society is the behavior of their contemporaries" (1970:31). "In class societies in which there is a high expectation of mobility, problems of *generation conflict* are endemic" (ibid.: 41, my italics). "Today, suddenly, because all the peoples of the world are part of one electronically based, intercommunicating culture, young people everywhere share a kind of experience that none of their elders ever had or will have . . . the break between the generations is wholly new; it is planetary and universal" (ibid.:63). Coleman and Hüsen (1985) proposed that the extension of formal schooling in Western societies, together with the increasing tendency for parents to work outside the home, creates an age segregation that makes the peer group, rather than the adult world, the major source of socialization during the high school years.

It was in the aftermath of the student disturbances in Berkeley, New York, Chicago, and Paris that the notion of the "generation gap" emerged into public consciousness. Certainly the violence of these demonstrations and the vehemence of the students' repudiation of the political and educational policies of the adult "establishment" lent support to the thesis that Friedenberg's view of adolescence as one of intractable generational conflict was correct. Blos, perhaps the preeminent contemporary psychoanalytic student of adolescence, says: "Generational conflict is essential for the growth of the self and of civilization" (1971:7).

In contrast, a number of observers have questioned the concept of a "generation gap." As indicated above, Offer's (1969) data strongly challenge this view; he reported that most normal adolescents shared their parents' values and, in most essentials, conformed to parental expectations in the conduct of their lives, in their goals and aspirations, and in their social and political opinions. Douvan and Adelson (1966) found no evidence for a "generation gap" among the junior high school students they surveyed. Keniston (1968, 1971) found that the "young radicals" he studied were, in most cases, expressing in an intensified form the liberal, antiauthoritarian views of their parents, who in many cases supported and encouraged their children's supposed "rebellion." Further, it soon became clear that only a small minority of the students at most institutions were involved in the takeovers, trashings, and protests that shook the campuses; the overwhelming majority of the students were at most passive supporters of, and often opposed to, the activities of the demonstrators. When Erikson (1975) speaks of the "revolt of humanist youth," he is describing the activities of certain late-adolescent students at Harvard and other high prestige colleges—a group of mostly affluent young people who in their concern with social and political issues and left-liberal orientation are highly atypical of most American young people at that time or since.

The weight of evidence, therefore, seems to argue against the existence of a true "generation gap." As Hill and Mönks put it, "the so-called generation gap is much exaggerated" (1977:18). In point of fact, most adolescents in most cultures conform rather quietly to the expectations of their elders. Sinha (1965) says that Indian adolescents do not show any aggression or disobedience toward parents; in ascribing their acceptance of and surrender to "fate" to a "pregenital fixation" to oral dependency, he appears, however, to be using the traditional Western-based psychoanalytic construction of "normal" adolescent behavior as his model.

[ 29 ]

From the previously mentioned normal population studies one gains a picture of general compliance and identification with adult standards, with, perhaps, brief and sporadic flurries of rebelliousness around nonessential issues. Indeed, the logic of cultural continuity demands that this be so; were each generation truly to reject or rebel against the values and ideologies of its parents, only chaos could result (Esman 1977).

Much has been made, too, of the "idealism" of adolescents. By this is meant, it would seem, the tendency of many young people to think in utopian terms, to conceive the world in the manner that Erikson (1975) calls "totalistic," and to imagine, as did some in the 1960s, that they could, through a kind of Children's Crusade, transform the world into a prelapsarian paradise, free of aggression, pollution, and inequality. Adelson (1975) points out, however, that in fact adolescents demonstrate no more "idealism" than anyone else. What they do demonstrate, he says, is a powerful strain of moralism; they tend to reduce complex political and social issues to moral ones or, as Erikson says, "to think ideologically—that is with an egocentric, narcissistic orientation determined to adapt the world to itself" (1975:204). True idealism, Adelson says, is a rare quality found, perhaps, in some postadolescents who have attained one of the higher levels of moral development as described by Kohlberg (1984).

Such moral judgment, Kohlberg says, is dependent in turn on the attainment of what Piaget called "formal operational thought," characterized by the capacity to think propositionally and to deal with abstract concepts. Piaget appears to have believed that this capacity was, at least potentially, a developmental universal; on the other hand, he clearly recognized that environmental circumstance could clearly affect its emergence:

> It is probable that in underdeveloped societies . . . the individual remains throughout his entire life at the level of concrete operations, without ever reaching the level of formal or propositional operations which are characteristic of adolescence in our cultural environment . . . in our societies the as yet unresolved question is whether these intellectual transformations exercise a similar effect on all classes of society. Certain indices would seem to show that they do not. . . . (1969:25–26)

In fact, Dulit (1972) has shown that even in a population of exceptionally gifted urban adolescents in a competitive and stimulating school, only 75 percent demonstrate the capacity for formal operational thought; among intellectually average older adolescents only 20–35 percent demonstrated this capacity. Since, as Kohlberg says, "advanced moral reasoning depends upon advanced logical reasoning" (1984:171), "idealism" and advanced conceptions of social justice are not likely to flourish in such soil.

From the body of data derived from the study of normal adolescents in the range of industrialized societies it appears, then, that the classical picture of *Sturm und Drang* is an inaccurate one—or, at least, that it describes only a minor, rather than the major, segment of the adolescent population. This is not intended to minimize the stressful character of adolescence in developed and developing societies. The young person traversing this phase is confronted by a number of crucial developmental "tasks" requiring major adaptations in many aspects of life. He must experience and adapt to the biological changes of puberty, with its attendant impact on the body and drive organization. He must learn to deal with new patterns of social relationships, tinged as they are increasingly with sexual feelings and fantasies and the definition of sexual role patterns. The adolescent must also undergo significant changes in his relations with parents and other family members, as he tests out his capacity for autonomous living while learning to come to terms with residual dependent wishes and feelings of attachment to parents who are no longer seen as omnipotent, idealized figures (Esman 1982). Decisions must be made about future life plans, particularly in areas of education and vocation, involving identification with actual or fantasized models.

Most adolescents, even in our society, seem to have developed during their "latency" years coping capacities (or "ego resources") that permit them to undergo a rather quiet transition from childhood to adulthood, marked by mild rebelliousness regarding some outward trappings of independence in early adolescence and with transitory moodiness with depressive undertones as they live through the transposition of their principal attachments from parents to age-mates. The presence of two supportive parents who are themselves able to adapt progressively to their adolescent's growth seems clearly to facilitate such an equable transition. The flamboyant behaviors of the minority, whether rebellious, delinquent, hypersexual, or merely noisy, provide for adult minds an ideal focus for the projection of their own imperfectly repressed or renounced impulses; it is then the "younger generation" that becomes the repository for these "bad" parts of the self (Anthony 1969).

It is true, nonetheless, that the adolescent whose development deviates in one way or another from the prevailing norms of his culture or subculture is likely to experience significant subjective distress. In *Black Boy*, Richard Wright (1945) depicted with great autobiographical sensitivity the plight of a black adolescent growing up as a bookish intellectual in a conventionally racist southern town in the 1920s. Seen not only as a deviant but as a threat to the established order, he was met with suspicion and hostility that, however disturbing at the time, drove him to escape to the North and to an environment in which his talents and interests could find a more fertile soil in which to flourish. His story is an intensified version of the commonplace experience of the intellectual adolescent of any class or color in most American public high schools even today—likely to be seen as a "nerd" (unless he is simultaneously a "jock") subject to social ostracism or exclusion from the "in" crowd until he is able in college to find a group with similar interests into which he can successfully integrate himself. Needless to say, the sympathetic support of parents and other adults can serve to mitigate the pain of such an adjustment.

We are speaking here of the unusual, the exceptional case. Where, however, a substantial proportion of the adolescent population deviates from this normative model, one is, I believe, entitled to assume a major disruption in the fabric of society at large—a disruption that is reflected in the behaviors and internal experiences of that group that is on the front lines of social change. As Hill and Mönks state it, " 'storm and stress,' 'rebelliousness' and the 'generation gap' are not universal phenomena and so they do not provide a very sound basis for discussions of [normal] adolescent development" (1977:6).

# 3

# Culture as Shaper of Adolescence

The influence of culture on adolescent thought and behavior can be conceptualized in two ways: 1) variations of the formal patterns of such phenomena as seen cross-culturally (synchronic); 2) the modifications of such patterns within a society as cultural changes occur (diachronic). In a sense these perspectives fall within the purview of, respectively, ethnology and sociology. Mead's reports of "growing up" and "coming of age" in exotic cultures have made the former widely familiar, while Hollingshead's "Elmtown" studies (1949, 1975) exemplify the latter. Above all, works of imaginative literature in the form of the

*Bildungsroman* or barely fictionalized reminiscences (typical of the "first novel") provide further perspectives.

Of these, perhaps the greatest, certainly the most evocative of time, place, and culture, is Joyce's *Portrait of the Artist as a Young Man*. Joyce brilliantly and touchingly portrays the torments of a boy tortured by his guilt-laden sexual longings in a priest-ridden Catholic society. Stephen Dedalus' terrors about the hellfire that awaited him after masturbation and his mingled triumph and shame after his first encounter with a prostitute were surely typical for adolescent boys in turn-of-the-century Dublin—all the more so at a time when the popular and "scientific" literature were everywhere virtually unanimous in their insistence on the moral evils and medical risks associated with masturbation.

Thus Hall (1904) refers to masturbation consistently as "unnatural," "scourge of the human race," a "disease," "this perversion," "evil," and "the vice" of which the majority of adolescents are, unfortunately, "guilty." Masturbation stunts the growth, impairs the heredity, lowers self-esteem, and induces depression, epilepsy, "sluggishness of heart action and circulation," cowardice, egotism, and innumerable other ills to which, unfortunately, the flesh is heir. Indeed, even Freud (1895), in his early theories of neurosogenesis, stressed the role of masturbation in the etiology of what he called "the actual neuroses." Freud shared, that is, the view of Hall and the medical "experts" of time that the "psychaesthenias" and "anxiety neuroses" were the result of "abnormal" sexual practices, chief among them masturbation. Hall was correct in his contention that masturbation led to lowering of self-esteem and feelings of shame; he merely failed to recognize the intervening variable of the sort of misinformation and moralism that he, like the other "authorities" of the time, introduced into the casual chain.

It was in such a cultural climate that Joyce (and, of course, innumerable other gifted adolescents) grew to maturity. Joyce succeeded, at least externally, in escaping it in order to "forge in the smithy of my soul the uncreated conscience of my race." For many who lacked his genius and his drive, however, a pall of guilt, shame, and fear lay over their emergent sexual lives through their adolescence and beyond.*

There is virtually universal agreement among social scientists that the phenomenology of adolescence—its duration, its behavioral characteristics, its place in family and social organization—is in large measure culturally determined. "Adolescence as we know it in modern societies is a creature of the industrial revolution and it continues to be shaped by the forces which defined that revolution: industrialization, specialization, urbanization, rationalization and bureaucratization of human organizations and institutions, and continuing technological development" (Hill and Mönks 1977:14–15). The image of the adolescent that emerges from the psychoanalytic and related literature—the experimentalist struggling toward the achievement of a sense of personal autonomy and individuation and a sexual relationship based on romantic love—is bound to that culture. As Baumrind says, "personal autonomy and individuation are

---

* The problem has been particularly acute for Irish adolescents and youth because of the tradition, based in large measure on economic factors, family structure, and the church's opposition to contraception, of late marriage and childbearing.

not universally accepted defining characteristics of the mature person, a fact that American behavioral scientists are prone to overlook" (1975:118).

In fact, the definition of a "mature person" is itself widely variable; this, in turn, contributes to the at times bewildering variety of criteria for the end of social adolescence. As Sebald (1984) points out, in rural Ireland a male is not considered an adult until his father dies; this cultural pattern is sharply dramatized in Synge's *The Playboy of the Western World*, in which the protagonist, by falsely claiming that he has killed his father, achieves the admiration of the crowd and the love of a beautiful woman—until his lie is discovered. Equally, in rural Greece a male must arrange for the dowries of his sisters before he achieves the status of a "man" and can proceed to his own courtship and marriage. These mores in traditional societies differ widely from those of many preliterate cultures, in which full adult status, both social and sexual, is attained upon completion of the initiation rites that mark the transition—and often the rebirth— out of childhood.

Even the forms of sexual adolescence are cast in the mold of culture. The more or less exclusive heterosexuality that is normative and idealized in Western societies, particularly those dominated by Christian morality, stands in sharp contrast to the institutionalized homoeroticism of young males in classical Athenian culture. More striking, however, is the pattern described by Stoller and Herdt (1982) among the Sambia of New Guinea. In this culture boys remain with their mothers well into middle childhood; fathers are distant, engaged in hunting, warriorhood, and ritual. At the first initiation, which occurs between 7 and 10, the boys are abruptly separated from their mothers and begin their indoctrination into the world of men, actively—and at times brutally—encouraged to identify with their fathers' male roles. At this time the young boy begins to suck older boys' penises, in order to accumulate the semen that, the Sambia believe, will make him a man. At puberty he changes roles and becomes the one whose penis is sucked by younger boys. Finally in his late teens he marries and becomes actively, aggressively, and exclusively heterosexual. This homoerotic behavior of late childhood and adolescence is culturally normative and is experienced as an aspect of acquiring masculine identity, of becoming like the father and assuming his social and sexual role. Remarkably, a mode of mutual male sexual gratification that is anathematized in Western societies is here raised to the level of a cultural imperative, buttressed by a belief system that, however bizarre to the Western scientific mind, achieves for those who hold it sufficient internal coherence and plausibility to provide a rationale for this unique approach to the process of becoming a man.

Becoming a woman is, of course, also a process shaped by cultural rituals and mores. Muensterberger cites the instance of the Nandi in Central Africa who, at least in earlier times, imposed on pubertal girls a system of elaborate rites that culminated in the excision of the clitoris by cauterization with a red-hot coal. This operation, conducted by a woman initiator and accepted without complaint, was followed by a period of isolation and enforced inactivity "in order to [make the girl] round and voluptuous and more desirable when she is married" (1961:362). (Note here the variation from current Western criteria for female "desirability.") In his classic description of Gikuyu culture, Jomo Kenyatta places this ritual procedure at the center of a whole program of *rites de passage,* which he considered a *"condi-tio sine qua non* of the whole teaching of tribal law, religion and morality" (n.d.: 128). In other cultures (notably feudal Europe) the girl's entrance into sexual adolescence was ef-fected by the *droit de seigneur* or *jus primae noctis,* in which the lord—or more often an older male relative—maintained and exercised the prerogative of "initiating" all new nubile females. (The plot of Beaumarchais' [and Mo-zart's] *Marriage of Figaro* hinges on Count Almaviva's am-bivalence about relinquishing this—by now outmoded—right.)

## The Question of "Youth Culture"

Along with the concept of the "generation gap" there arose, in the middle years of this century, the notion of a special "youth culture," standing in opposition to and definable from the prevailing and dominant adult culture throughout the Western industrialized world.

Margaret Mead (1970) was a major spokesman for this position, contending, as noted earlier, that the advances in technology and, especially, in the communication and transmission of information of the postwar years made the experience of young people qualitatively different from that of their elders. Coleman (1961) spoke of "the adolescent society," contending that the conditions of life at midcen-tury, including universal secondary education, engendered the peer culture that served as the primary agent of sociali-zation for many, if not most, adolescents. The socializing role of parents and teachers has, in this view, waned appre-ciably, all the more so as the two parent family becomes the exception, as mothers are increasingly out of the home, and as teachers are seen as time-serving disciplinarians rather than as models for emulation. Thus Gottlieb, Reeves, and Ten Houten stated that "school becomes the center where the adolescent comes to focus on his peer group as a vital reference point" and where adolescents are "introduced to a variety of ideas that may be in conflict with the ideas and values held by their parents" (1966:x).

Marxist analysis offers another variation on this theme. As the means of production become ever more rationalized and mechanized, the labor of children and young persons becomes not only inessential but counterproductive. Thus in a preindustrial economy such as that of India, child labor not only survives but is often the economic mainstay of the family (Jackman and Valli 1988). Contrariwise, the abolition of child labor in the industrialized world is seen as determined not solely by humanitarian motives, but also (even primarily) by the need to keep young persons out of the labor force so that adults can maintain gainful employment. The result, however, is that "youth is not central to the economy and has become isolated as a dependent economic liability" (Brake 1985:25). It is the marginal status of adolescents in modern industrial culture—their exclusion from participation in central aspects of society, their possession of fewer rights, and their exercise of fewer responsibilities—that leads, says Mahler (1977), to tension and a sense of society as belonging only to adults. The resentment thus engendered may lead to behaviors—antisocial, dissocial, or "utopian"—that are perceived by adults as deviant and rebellious.

On the other hand, Hollingshead (1975) perceives the essential features of youth subcultures as learned behaviors acquired by identification, with an internalization of attitudes and values of the family and other significant persons. Thus in his view, children from classes I–III (upper and middle class) are taught to be good and minimize aggression by means of controlled and supervised play, while class V (lower class) children, though "told to be good," are uncontrolled and unsupervised by absent or overwhelmed parents; their behavior is "unacceptable" by middle class standards by the time they get to school. In other words, their adolescent behavior is simply a continuation of patterns learned in early childhood and is not explainable simply as a manifestation of adolescence per se. Similarly, Kandel and Lesser found no evidence to support the concept of a "youth society." "In critical areas," they say, "interactions with peers support, express and specify for the peer context the values of parents and other adults; and the adolescent sub-culture is coordinated with, and in fact is a particular expression of, the culture of the larger society" (1972:168). "There is no doubt," they add, "that with respect to future life goals, in both countries [the United States and Denmark] parental influence is stronger than peer influence" (ibid.:183).

Whether a matter of adult perception or of "objective" reality, however, certain adolescent and youthful behaviors are so flamboyant and so widely diffused as to suggest the existence of a number of definable subcultures. A brief weekend visit to London's Trafalgar Square, for instance, would yield an intense impression of black clad youth of both sexes parading varicolored coiffures, elaborately sculpted in the manner of "primitive" tribes. A French journalist (Muller 1988) proclaims the advent on the continent of the Skinheads—violent adolescents and "youths" of the kind that in England descend on soccer matches and, disinhibited by large quantities of beer ("lager louts"), provoke violent and, at times, fatal fights with the supporters of opposing teams. Los Angeles has for years been plagued by large violent gangs of black and Hispanic adolescents who have at times engaged in random shooting sprees, most recently in upper middle class neighborhoods (Mari 1988).

It is tempting to perceive these phenomena as diversified manifestations of a particular malaise of our time. Sebald (1984) reminds us, however, that in 1857 the state militia was called out to quell the violence of adolescent gangs on the streets of New York City and that, according to Macaulay, youthful gang behavior was rife in seventeenth-century London; indeed, one of the more violent gangs of the period was known as the Mohawks. And as noted earlier, Shakespeare depicts in *Romeo and Juliet* the "turf" war of Veronese adolescents in the late Middle Ages. Even before the industrial revolution, it would appear that urbanization and its attendant evils—poverty and family disorganization among them—generated some of the features of adolescent subcultures with which we have become familiar.

But there is general agreement among social scientists that as a fixed star on the social horizon, "youth societies" are a product of industrialization. Indeed, the very concept of "youth" can be seen as a metaphor for social change. This can be seen most sharply in the developing nations of the so-called third world, in which rapid (if chaotic) industrialization is coupled with a large population of late adolescents with rising expectations but only modest prospects for fulfillment. The political ferment of these youth groups —generally identified as "students"—has led to major revolutionary change in many such societies and threatens (or promises) to do so in others. Mainland China is only the latest illustration of this phenomenon; here rapid industrialization and economic liberalization, along with in-creased exposure to Western cultural and political ways, has fueled a demand for parallel political liberalization among students and other youth groups, leading to the extraordi-nary and tragic popular uprising of May 1989.

Gillis (1973) has effectively delineated the contrasts and convergences between two "youth cultures" of the early twentieth century—specifically those of English and Ger-man adolescents between 1900 and 1933. In Britain, a rising middle class evolved, through a "disciplined compromise" with a traditional aristocracy, a patriotic, highly structured, conformist, and moralistic youth movement known as the Boy Scouts. At the same time the less secure German bour-geoisie, despised by the militaristic elite, generated the Wandervögel, the rebellious bohemian antiauthoritarian youth who proved to be the prototype for the "turbulent" adolescent described as normative by the early psychoana-lysts from their Central European perspective. Different as they appear to be, however, both movements were similar in the way they recognized and institutionalized the depen-dent and the essentially passive position of a growing seg-ment of the young population who, no longer economically essential, were not deemed ready for and were excluded from full adult status in their societies.

The emergence of contemporary "youth cultures" has prob-ably been more clearly drawn and certainly more thor-oughly studied in post–World War II Britain than in any other society. Since 1945 a steady stream of youth styles and subcultures has emerged—predominantly male, exclusively working class—Teddy boys, mods, rockers, punks, Skinheads, each with its own transitory sets of folkways, modes of dress, hairstyles, and music preferences. Despite their superficial variety, they serve to illustrate the basic principles that appear to underlie the emergence of such subgroups within the broader frame of national and international cultures.

"Culture," say Clarke, Hill, Jefferson, and Roberts, "is the way the normal social relations of a group are structured and shaped; it is also the way these shapes are experienced, understood and interpreted" (1975:11). The culture of postwar Britain has been dominated by two overriding realities —the collapse of imperial power (and the attendant loss of national self-esteem) and the collapse of the British industrial economy, with the emergence of a subclass of chronically unemployed and unemployable young men (with its attendant loss of individual self-esteem). As the dominant middle class culture has become increasingly affluent and, at least in the Southeast, dominated by bourgeois consumer values, these marginal working class youths have sought for and found ever newer ways of maintaining self-esteem, by seeking either to deny, negate, or flaunt their marginality. In a society in which class structures remain stubbornly inflexible, the persistent features of life as a working class youth—unemployment or dead-end jobs at low pay, educational disadvantage, routinization of labor, and loss of skills —are experienced as humiliating, even emasculating. When, Delors (1977) points out, the majority of young people are obliged to accept unskilled work offering little prospect of a career, work ceases to be a basis for self-esteem or for affiliation. (This can be seen in the United States, too, among

the young people who can find work only in fast-food res-
taurants in jobs totally lacking in prestige or any sense of
accomplishment.)

To defend against the sense of institutionalized castra-
tion and to ward off the depressive feelings associated with
the loss of self-esteem and alienation, working class adolescents and youth have evolved a sequence of what Brake
(1985) has called "magical" defensive efforts, from the Ed-
wardian dress of the postwar Teddy boys to the caricatured
hypermasculinity of the Skinheads and "lager louts." In the
words of Clarke et al., they " 'solve,' in an imaginary way,
problems which at the concrete material level remain un-
solved."

Thus the Teddy boy expropriation of an upper class style
of dress "covers the gap between largely manual, unskilled,
nearly lumpen real careers and life chances and the 'all
dressed up and nowhere to go' experience of Saturday eve-
ning" (ibid.:72). As Dixon puts it, "they act, not as if they
were on holiday, but as if they were an advertisement for
holidays" (Frith and Horne 1987:182). For, as Clarke et al.
point out, there is no "sub-cultural solution" to the real
problems of the young working class male in contemporary
British society.

For adolescents growing up in the dominant middle class
culture, the situation is somewhat more subtle and complex. The life of the middle class adolescent in Western
society is shaped by and serves to reflect deep-seated trends
in the economic and moral crises of contemporary capitalism—trends that are spreading even into the "socialist"
world as it seeks to improve the lot of its citizens by adopt-
ing "capitalist" principles. According to Daniel Bell, the
culture of modern capitalism "is one of self-expression and

self-gratification. It is anti-institutional and antinomian, in that the individual is taken to be the measure of satisfaction, and *his* feelings, sentiments and judgments, not some objective standard of quality and value, determine the worth of cultural objects" (1978:xvii). "For the last fifty years the economy has been geared to producing the life-style paraded by the culture" (ibid.:xxv). Thus "the character structure inherited from the 19th century, with its emphasis on self-discipline, delayed gratification and restraint . . . clashes sharply with the culture, where such bourgeois values have been completely rejected" (ibid.:37).

In the culture of late capitalism, that is, the primary role of the adult citizen is that of consumer and adolescence has become, more and more, a training for the assumption of that role. The nineteenth-century values of which Bell speaks are, it should be noted, the values that have informed and continue to inform psychoanalysis and its view of the healthy personality. They are enshrined in Erikson's epigenetic sequence of developmental achievements, which include such "virtues" as autonomy, industry, generativity, and wisdom. These "virtues" seem, however, less and less relevant in a culture that prizes above all self-gratification and in which, Bell says, "more and more individuals want to be identified not by their occupational base but by their cultural tastes and life-styles" (ibid.:38). As the *London Sunday Times* (1988) puts it, "shop till you drop on the Michelin Mile." In a culture dominated by a "fun" morality, the old values do not hold; psychoanalysis is increasingly seen as irrelevant.

Training for consumerism begins, of course, well before adolescence. At the very least it begins with the child's exposure to television and the relentless barrage of commercial messages it purveys. In the past forty years television has become the primary educative and socializing instrument of the culture. The average child in the United States and Britain devotes as much time to watching TV as to school attendance—indeed, more, since on weekends and holidays he or she may devote the entire waking day to it— and if the medium has one message, that message is "consume."

By the time they become adolescents these children not only have begun their own careers as consumers, but have acquired a significant influence on the consumption patterns and preferences of their parents.* If they are girls they have become the targets of a vast literature of style and fashion journals, fan magazines, and "life-style" periodicals, all geared toward the promotion and shaping of their consuming habits. Thus in 1979 80 percent of all American adolescents went to the movies at least once a week and 50 percent owned and used cameras and over 50 percent of adolescent girls bought phonograph records (*Media Book* 1979). In fact, the popular music business depends for its very life on the consuming habits of adolescents. Popular music accounts for over 90 percent of all records produced, and the bulk of these are bought by adolescent girls. The industry has therefore developed highly sophisticated marketing strategies that astutely capitalize on well recognized aspects of adolescent development. The prototypical popular music performer, particularly in the rock genre, is a late adolescent or postadolescent male who adopts the stance of a rebel against conventional adult mores (long hair, bizarre and/or "macho" dress, the use of street language, ostentatious use of drugs) designed to appeal to and vicariously

* A Denver bank has recently begun issuing a special credit card for 12– 15 year olds.

gratify the phallic narcissism of young adolescent males. "The trick," says the English social critic George Melly, "is to shift the emphasis so that the pop idol, originally representing a masculine rebel, is transformed into a masturbation-fantasy object for adolescent girls" (1970:40). In short, Melly concludes, "what starts as revolt finishes as style" (ibid.:43).

A product of this marketing strategy was the "teeny-bopper" culture that grew up on the periphery of the rock music world during the sixties and seventies. It consisted of preadolescent and early adolescent girls who attached themselves, in fantasy or in actuality, to male rock groups and individual performers. Their devotion, though generally restricted to passionate crushes (Melly's "masturbation fantasy"), frequently included making themselves available for overt sexual activity. Needless to say, an industry that purveyed posters, buttons, and T-shirts—the panorama of modern kitsch objects—grew up to serve the "needs" of this nubile subculture.

McRobbie and Garber found that the "teeny-bopper" culture owed its efflorescence to its ability to fulfill a multiplicity of such needs. Although it represents an enactment of a quasi-sexual ritual, it can be accommodated to the home as well as being expressed in the public arena of the rock concert. No qualifications are required—anyone can join; no special skills are demanded; wealth and appearance are not factors. And identification with the socially deviant models serves to express in encapsulated form a rebellion against conventional values, while permitting continued conformity at school and in other normative settings. Above all, however, the teeny-bopper posture involves the girl in the living out of a highly conventionalized feminine role—

that of the adoring female in awe of an idealized male. "The small structured and highly manufactured space that is available for 10–15 year old girls to create a personal and autonomous area seems to be offered only on the understanding that these strategies also symbolize a future general subordination—as well as a present one" (1975:221). Ironically, the rock world, ostensibly an expression of youthful rebelliousness, maintains the traditional double standard, in which the female performer is almost invariably relegated to the role of a singing sex object intoning lyrics of romantic longing.

The impact on adolescence of culture and cultural change is nowhere more dramatically demonstrated than in the psychopathological variant known as anorexia nervosa. For generations after its first description by Gull (1874) it remained a relatively rare disorder, affecting white middle-class adolescent girls and young women. Today the picture is vastly different. Anorexia nervosa, along with its companion disorder, bulimia, has become a plague of the young generation of women of a wide range of social and class backgrounds. Recently reports of cases in black women have been increasingly frequent (Pumereiga, Edwards, and Mitchell 1984). Thus from a rather obscure illness known primarily to physicians anorexia nervosa has become a staple of popular journalistic interest, with frequent newspaper and television coverage.

One is pressed to search for explanations of this fact in the sociocultural sphere, and one finds little difficulty in doing so. Young women in our society—and this appears to be a universal feature of industrialized nations—are exposed to no message more clearly and unremittingly re-peated than that of the urgent necessity for social and sex-ual success of being thin. The canon of female beauty has undergone a radical transformation over the generations, from the fleshy ideals of sixteenth-century Venice and sev-enteenth-century Flanders (as represented in the Venuses of Titian and Rubens) to that of the current elongated, pencil thin fashion model prototypes featured in popular litera-ture. The slogan "You can't be too rich or too thin" epito-mizes the values of a society in which the best selling non-fiction book for many weeks was *Thinner Thighs in Thirty Days*. The magazines read by adolescent girls are dominated by articles on the latest fads in weight reduction and by advertisements featuring photographs of manikins who are promoted, along with the equally emaciated institutional-ized anorectics, the ballet dancers, as models for emulation and identification. Both among peers and at home the girl who fails to conform to this distorted ideal is likely to be teased and criticized—made, as a patient remembers having being made, to feel that she could not possibly be loved by her weight-conscious parents or accepted by her peers if she were "fat." The result has been what Rakoff has called the "democratization of the disorder"—once the monopoly of the rich and well-favored, but now the common property of all classes but the very poor in our affluent and well-fed society. More significantly, however, we have seen the dis-persion of a set of values and attendant behaviors fueled by commercial interests.

Still another example of the acute susceptibility of ado-lescents to cultural—that is, economic—pressures is the pattern of tobacco use. As is well known, smoking was primarily a masculine habit until early in this century;

Wolf-Ferrari's light opera *The Secret of Suzanne* exemplifies the surreptitiousness of female smoking in the late Victorian era, when smoking—or at least public smoking—was the mark of a "loose" woman or demimondaine. In the wake of the feminist movement of the past thirty years and in the face of growing male concern about the link between lung cancer and smoking, the tobacco industry has aggressively directed its message toward adolescent girls and young women with such slogans as "You've come a long way, baby" and with the production of "slim" and "light" cigarettes. The results are demonstrated in recent studies that show that both in the United States (Pirie, Murray, and Luepker 1988) and Italy (Monarca et al. 1987) the incidence of smoking among high school girls is significantly higher than in boys. A substantial change in cultural attitudes and in adolescent behavior is apparent.*

These illustrations of commercial manipulation should not be taken to suggest that all aspects of adolescent behavior or the patterns of youthful subcultures should be ascribed to marketing pressures. It is in the interaction of normal developmental forces, broad scale socioeconomic tendencies, and specific cultural influences that patterns of adolescent behavior and youth subcultures are forged. In particular, the characteristic modes of adolescent behavior in industrialized societies are a function of the tension between youthful aspiration and social possibility, between young people's desire for adult status and the marginality that their society imposes on them. To quote Frith:

* The ultimate in this appeal is that of a current cigarette advertisement extolling the virtues of "the slimmest of the slim," thus by implication encouraging both anorexia and cigarette smoking.

The problem ... is that the young since the nineteen twenties have come to symbolize leisure, to embody the good times. Youth seems to be freer than everyone else in society. ... they are not bound like their elders by the routines and relationships of family and career. But it is because they are not really free that this matters. The truth of youth culture is that the young displace to their free time the problems of work and family and future. It is because they lack power that the young account for their lives in terms of play, focus their politics on leisure. (Quoted in Brake 1985:189) (1983:200)

What Frith ignores here, however, is the fact that the very values he ascribes to youth have increasingly been those of the adult world itself—the pursuit of "fun," the hedonistic unconcern for the future, the loosening of sexual constraints, and the withdrawal from politics to sport. As Glassner and Coughlin point out, "Parsons ... noted that adolescents were expected to be irresponsible and to spend their time having fun, and that their values were expressive (e.g., popularity, attractiveness) rather than instrumental" (1987:261–262). In the forty years that have elapsed since Parsons made these observations, these have become the dominant values of the adult world in American culture.

## The Drug Culture in Contemporary Adolescence

The interpenetration of adolescence and culture is nowhere more evident than in the area of drug use. What had, in the years before World War II, been the special province of adolescents and young adults outside the mainstream of middle class society (primarily, that is, jazz musicians and their acolytes and young black and Hispanic men) emerged by the 1970s as normative behavior across the broad perspective of American society. Marijuana smoking became a rite of passage for middle class adolescents; for some it became and remained a significant part of their lives, although for most it came to occupy a less central, largely recreational role. Few, at least in the cities, escaped its influence entirely. More recently, cocaine has followed a similar, if less widespread, pattern of dispersion in the youthful population. Many adolescents seen in clinical settings, at any rate, have had some experience with it; in its cheap, highly addictive form known as "crack" it is widely thought to be at the root of recent outbreaks of violent crime, especially in the black and Hispanic communities.

The predominant drug of choice for adolescents—and adults—in the Western world is alcohol. Kandel (1975) has shown that substance use and abuse by adolescents in all cultures almost invariably begins with alcohol and tobacco, which may or may not then progress to other drugs. She has found, however, substantial crosscultural differences in patterns of abuse. In comparing American, French and Israeli adolescents, Kandel found that although similar patterns of alcohol use prevailed between American and French adolescents, "American adolescents had much higher rates of illicit drug use than adolescents in either of the other two countries" (Kandel 1984:282). At least twice as many French as Israeli youths used alcohol or tobacco, consistent with the long established fact that Israel has one of the lowest rates of alcoholism in the world; France one of the highest. Similarly, where 31 percent of French adolescents had used marijuana by age 18, only 8 percent of Israeli youths had done so. And where 26 percent of French adolescents acknowledged ever using an illicit drug, only 8 percent of Israelis did so; in contrast, 65 percent of American adolescents had admitted such experiences.

Thus the significance of substance use and abuse must be understood in the context of the wide range of variations among societies, even within the Western industrialized world. The ubiquity of wine and other fermented beverages in France is well-known, and a rather tolerant acceptance of alcoholism has been a characteristic French attitude. In contrast, Jews have traditionally limited wine consumption to ceremonial occasions, and drunkenness has been intensely stigmatized. These long-standing value positions are evidently important factors in the shaping of adolescent use of intoxicants of all kinds. The conformity of Israeli adolescents to these powerful cultural traditions would also seem to belie stereotypic notions about "adolescent rebellion."

Although popular attention and concern focused on the explosion of marijuana smoking among adolescents in the 1960s, it seemed clear to many that the pattern was set by the burgeoning use of psychoactive drugs of all kinds among adults during the same period. Indeed, many of the drugs that had their passing vogue among experimentally minded adolescents—barbiturates, amphetamines, Quaaludes, Valium—trickled down from the adult population that consumed them on prescription in ever growing quantities. The use of such hallucinogens as LSD and mescaline was promoted and propagandized to the adolescent world by such adult gurus as Timothy Leary and Richard Alpert, both, at the time, bearing Harvard faculty credentials. Marijuana also drifted down from the college to the high school to the junior high school population, just as tobacco smoking had done generations earlier, as the young sought to emulate their older siblings and other youthful role models.* Technology also played a significant role, as the expansion of air travel made the process of smuggling large supplies of cannabis easier, feeding and generating a rapidly expanding market in which supply and demand pursued each other in ever widening circles, frustrating all efforts at interdiction and control.

Changing cultural attitudes are apparent in the experience of any clinician who deals with adolescent patients. In the sixties and early seventies, many parents, discovering that their teenage children were experimenting with marijuana, anxiously brought them to the pediatrician or child psychiatrist for evaluation, concerned that their child might become—or already be—a confirmed addict (cf. Morgan 1981:159). Today's parents—many of them those same teenagers—take such experimentation as a matter of course, recognizing that, in the absence of signs of adaptive failure, it must be seen as part of the process of growing up in contemporary society. Today crack occupies the place that marijuana did a generation ago—a drug (clearly, of course, a more dangerous one) once primarily associated with minority populations, its appearance in white middle class homes arouses intense anxiety and generates clinical attention in short order.

Zinberg (1984) argues forcefully that much of the social concern about adolescent drug use is a product of the moralism inherent in American middle class culture—the moralism that gave us the "great experiment" of prohibition and that fails to distinguish between experimental, recreational *use* of psychoactive substances and habitual, com-

* Marijuana "gained some cachet through association with the artistic and intellectual rebels of the 1950s" (Morgan 1981:159).

pelled, uncontrolled *abuse* of these drugs. The former, he maintains, represents little actual cost to society, while the latter constitutes a major social problem and should be the appropriate locus of public concern. The official policy of total legal proscription tends to discourage, rather than encourage controlled use and leaves adolescents to seek guidance from peers who, though they may have their own sanctions and rituals, tend to be less reliable guides than adults might be. And in any case, the official hypocrisy that condones the use of alcohol, the abuse of which imposes social costs far beyond those of most other "recreational" drugs, is not lost on American adolescents.

Typically adults, including many mental health professionals, assume that adolescent drug use represents a "rebellion" against adult social standards. As Zinberg points out, however:

> The second generation of users tries the illicit drug not primarily because it wants to rebel against the straight society . . . but out of curiosity or because they are interested in its effects. . . . By this time even the straight society has moved away from its formerly rigid position and has become mainly confused. Such confusion encourages others . . . who are not primarily motivated by either drug hunger or social rebellion to experiment with the drug. (1984:189)

Glassner and Coughlin found that, like their non-using subjects, adolescent drug users had highly conventional values and "give visions of the future that are highly conventional" (1987:222). "The social order is accepted and its values largely unquestioned . . . their general orientation to the adult world . . . is neither hostile nor alienated" (ibid.:206–207). Williams (1989), in his study of a teenage cocaine ring, similarly found that his subjects, despite their immersion in a deviant, degraded, and illicit subculture, conform in many ways with conventional values, including a strong work ethic and an aspiration toward bourgeois standards of social achievement. They have found a way to achieve pride of performance and status in a world that offers them little opportunity to do so through "legitimate" channels. Even their disposition to violence can be seen as scarcely deviant in a gun-ridden society that, through television, exposes its children to thousands of murders, beatings, robberies, and other brutalities during their five or six hours each day before the small screen. Unfortunately, those who use the product they distribute, made vulnerable by the same social handicaps, are driven further into the subculture of social deviance.

The values of the dominant adult culture impose themselves on adolescents in other situations that to the superficial observer appear to represent typical adolescent issues and (mis)behaviors. A recent case in point is that of five middle class adolescent boys who were accused of sexually abusing a 17-year-old mentally retarded girl while eight male peers stood by and cheered them on. Several of these boys were star athletes—captains of the football and baseball teams at their local high school. Remarkably, expressions of outrage by students and adults in the community were as often directed at the girl and her defenders as against the boys who allegedly perpetrated the offense. One student reported receiving death threats from the "friends" of the accused boys, while many adults expressed concern primarily that publicity about the case would reflect badly on the community. What appeared to some to be an adolescent sexual prank, a piece of adolescent "acting out," exposed a system of community values that distinctly favored sexually aggressive male athletes over handicapped females and, characteristically, tended to place blame on the victim.

The boys' high status as "jocks" thus tended to make them immune to criticism in the eyes not only of their adolescent classmates, but in those of many adults in a community steeped in the American idealization of the athlete. This mirrored a series of recent reports of deceptive practices by colleges and universities that were paying nominally "amateur" student athletes or carrying them as legitimate students despite deficient or nonexistent academic performance. It further reflected the disproportionate economic rewards accorded to professional athletes, a measure of the society's conception of relative merit and cultural status.

Finally, the cultural legitimization of violence appears in sharp relief in recent incidents of racially inspired attacks on young black males who have invaded the "turf" of working class white ethnic populations. Young males, predominantly late adolescents, with attitudes shaped by the traditional suspiciousness and territoriality of their immigrant elders and living in narrow enclaves that tend to perpetuate these attitudes, often feel bound to enforce such territorial restrictions, even at gunpoint, in order to validate their masculinity as subculturally defined. (The symbolic meaning of the gun and the baseball bat need scarcely be belabored here.) Adult members of these communities are quick to rise to the defense of their violent youths—not only out of family loyalty, but because these young men are carrying into action the prejudices and fears their parents feel and articulate but may not express in overt acts.

# 4

# Adolescence and "The New Sexuality"

The changes in sexual behavior that have characterized the past three decades have been designated by some observers as a "sexual revolution." Assuming the existence of such a "revolution," we should expect adolescents, experimental in outlook and caught up in the process of adaptation to their newly acquired sexual capacities, to be its shock troops and to be engaged in the energetic formulation of a new sexual morality. We must also expect, however, that many of those who cannot or

This chapter is an expanded and revised version of a chapter from T. B. Karasu and C. W. Socarides, eds., *On Sexuality: Psychoanalytic Observations*. New York International Universities Press, 1979.

will not participate in the revolutionary enterprise will experience serious conflict, made the more poignant by the flamboyance of their peers, and that they will themselves develop institutionalized ways of coping with this situation.

The study of adolescent sexuality is fraught with difficulties. The task of distinguishing between overt behavior and inner attitudes is equaled in difficulty only by that of assessing the various meanings that may be expressed by identical behaviors. Offer and his associates (1969) have alerted us to the problem of overgeneralization and extrapolation from clinical phenomena to those of normal development. Clinical study may, however, demonstrate the special stresses imposed by new developments and some of the defensive and adaptive responses elaborated by those who are vulnerable to such stresses; these may to a lesser degree be characteristic ones for the population at large. A survey of the response of adolescents to the "new sexuality" requires, therefore, a multifaceted approach, employing both social science and clinical methods to arrive at useful conclusions.

Historically, adolescents in our culture have inhabited a narrow and shifting ground defined by their own intense sexual urges, on the one hand, and the constraints imposed upon them by social norms, conventions, and moral judgments, on the other. Prime among these constraints has been the Judeo-Christian tradition, which bans or frowns upon all sexual activities other than genital congress in the setting of monogamous marriage. In this context all sexual avenues open to adolescents have been potentially—and often actually—burdened with guilt and/or shame and every adolescent engaged in them has been obliged to make some accommodation to this burden (cf. Gadpaille 1977). In an earlier work (Esman 1972) I described some of the ways in which this was done, in which, that is, the adolescent's superego was reshaped in response to the new needs and possibilities opened to him by his sexual maturation. Mead's study of Samoan adolescents (1928) claims to show that such conflicts are neither inevitable nor universal, but that they are embedded in a particular cultural matrix.

The "new sexuality" appears to represent a significant, if not quite revolutionary, change in cultural patterns. Many of the values and attitudes characteristic of the older tradition seem to have crumbled along with the institutions that embodied and supported them. The form and content of this "new morality" have been extensively documented. Illustrative is the study by Wall and Kaltreider (1977) of adult patients in an outpatient gynecology clinic in California. Comparison with similar studies performed by Kinsey et al. (1953) and Winokur, Guze, and Pfeiffer (1959) makes evident striking shifts in attitudes and behavior; Wall and Kaltreider found "a substantial decrease in formal marriage, a reduction in the wish for children, . . . and an attitudinal shift toward acceptance of a bisexual adaptation" (1977:565).

Evidence of the impact of these changes upon adolescents has been increasingly prominent in the social science literature. Sorensen, for example, reports that in his large national sample 19 percent of 13 to 15-year-old girls agreed with the statement "if you really dig a boy it's all right to have sex with him even if you've only known him for a few hours"; 53 percent of all adolescent boys shared a similar sentiment regarding girls. He defines what he calls "the new sexual relationship—serial monogamy without marriage" as "a close sexual relationship of uncertain duration between two unmarried adolescents from which either party may depart when he or she desires, often to participate in another such relationship" (1973:219). Twenty-one percent of all American adolescents were at the time of his survey involved in such an arrangement (as were 23 percent of Wall and Kaltreider's subjects). Some 62 percent of all adolescents surveyed said, "So far as sex is concerned, I do what I want to do regardless of what society thinks." However, 30–35 percent of these subjects acknowledged that "sometimes I feel guilty about my sexual behavior." (Interestingly, the highest percentage of these "guilty" ones were boys 13 to 15; presumably their guilt referred largely to masturbation.)

These attitudinal changes are reflected in actual behavior. Where only 5 percent of U.S. white females (and 12 percent of blacks) in the birth cohort 1944–1946 had initiated sexual activity by age 16, 18 percent of whites and 33 percent of blacks in the 1962–1964 cohort had done so (Hofferth, Kahn, and Baldwin 1987). Similar findings have been reported by Schmidt and Sigusch from West Germany, where the age of first coitus in comparable adolescent populations declined sharply between 1966 and 1970, especially among the more educated (gymnasium) students. The girls in the 1970 study had a "much greater sexual motivation for their first coitus and correspondingly the first coitus was more often the result of mutual initiative" than had been the case hitherto. Further, they "more often felt happier after the first coitus and less often found [it] unpleasant, repulsive and/or disgusting" (1972:41). Although similar trends obtained among boys, they were much less marked.

Peplau reported that women appear to determine both the occurrence and timing of intercourse in dating couples; "when a couple does not have intercourse, the woman's attitudes are usually the restraining force. It is clear that in couples not having intercourse the man is often highly desirous . . . the woman is not. . . . Women in couples who have intercourse are significantly more liberal in their sexual attitudes than are women in couples that abstain. For men there is no difference" (1977:33). For both men and women the double standard has virtually disappeared. The major change underlying the greater frequency and earlier age of onset of sexual intercourse must, then, be the attitudes and behavior of young women.

Further, among middle class adolescents in the New York Longitudinal Study population (Chess, Thomas, and Cameron 1976) few of the girls spoke of marriage and family as life goals; this confirms Hendin's (1975) observations in his study of Columbia University students. Finally, Yankelovich found in his 1973 survey that "fewer unmarried students (61 percent) personally look forward to getting married than in 1968 (66 percent)" (1974:59). Yankelovich's study is of further interest in demonstrating the spread of the "new morality" from the vanguard college population to the noncollege, traditionally more conservative group. In 1969, 43 percent of college students said that they would "welcome more acceptance of sexual freedom" while only 22 percent of the noncollege population echoed this view. By 1973, 47 percent of the noncollege youth took this position. Similar patterns were found in regard to questions about abortion, homosexuality, and premarital intercourse.

From these sociological studies, then, certain conclusions can reasonably be drawn: (1) A "new morality" developed in the adult world in the decades of the sixties and seventies, one that sanctions, if it does not encourage, a free sexuality among adolescents. (2) The predominant shift underlying the "new morality" has been in the values and behavior of adolescent girls, who now feel permitted to do what had earlier been forbidden them. It seems clear that this change is in large measure an outgrowth of the "new feminism." (3) The characteristic pattern of "new sexual behavior" is that of "serial monogamy." Promiscuity is not the rule and, indeed, appears to be found only among the more disturbed members of the youth population.

Clinical data may permit us a sharper perspective on these findings, giving us insight into both their extent and their boundaries. For example, Mary, when first seen at 15, was a shy, anxious girl who sought treatment because of her inability to relate to boys and express herself in school. Unusually pretty, she had many girlfriends, but had never gone out with a boy and felt paralyzed when approached by them. Further, she was getting mediocre grades in school, although unusually bright, because she couldn't bring herself to speak out in class and was profoundly anxious about examinations. Prim, a bit compulsive in dress and manner, she was shocked by the conduct of her one-year-younger sister who smoked marijuana and engaged in what Mary regarded as promiscuous sex. She soon became aware of her unconscious attachment to her idealized ne'er-do-well father who had left the family when she was nine, had remarried, and was living in another country. Her mother, hardworking, outwardly self-reliant but chronically depressed, represented an ambivalently valued ego-ideal figure for her.

Two years of intensive therapy led to considerable loosening of Mary's too rigid defenses. At 17, she met a bachelor neighbor some ten years her senior; in short order she entered into an intense romantic and sexual relationship with him—the first such attachment of her life. Her mother not only offered no objection to this liaison, but openly supported it. That Bill was a father surrogate was obvious. Mary ultimately moved in with him, enjoying for a year or so a part-lover, part-daughter role in which sex, though present, played a secondary part to being cared for, supported, and desired.

Gradually over the next year she became increasingly dissatisfied with Bill. He was too staid and compulsive, not sufficiently romantic, and indifferent to her expanding range of intellectual and cultural interests. Finally, in an act of courage and determination buttressed by feminist ideals of self-realization and autonomy, she broke with him, quickly finding a college classmate with whom she became intensely enamored and with whom she launched into a new and exciting sexual affair. She recognized that the relationship with Bill had perpetuated her preadolescent dependency and had, in fact, served as a defense against age-appropriate involvement and experimentation with her peers. The relative ease with which she had entered a pseudomature sexual affair was clearly facilitated by the current ethos (including, of course, the elimination of fears about impregnation), but it also enabled her to avoid uncomfortable social encounters with younger men.

Jonathan was sixteen when he sought treatment because of a series of terrifying LSD trips. He, like Mary, was the product of a broken home. Though still living together, his parents were completely estranged, and his father moved out and sought a divorce from his alcoholic wife about a year later. Jonathan was an intellectually gifted, aesthenic, and rather passive boy who, having done badly at two con-

ventional private schools, was in his senior year at a somewhat "special" school for bright but "different" adolescents,
like himself. He had already had a fairly extended sexual
relationship with one of his classmates, a girl with a similar
school history; they were both 14 when their affair began,
and it was still going on, sporadically. Jonathan wanted to
detach himself from Jennifer, but she was deeply attached
to him, and he, more or less submissively, accepted her
favors, along with those of one or two other girls who made
themselves available to him until he went off to college.

There he met Cecily, a confused young woman who became dependently attached to him so that when he dropped
out after a year and returned to New York she left with him
and, at her insistence, they moved into an apartment together. (Jonathan was now 19.) Again he submitted to an
arrangement that he found unpleasant, until he returned to
a local university a year later and was with great relief
obliged to move back to the family home. During the next
two years he was involved in fleeting and loveless sexual
contacts with girls he had known in high school and an
occasional new acquaintance. Sometimes, during periods
when he found girls unavailable, he considered and occasionally accepted homosexual overtures. He was clearly uncomfortable in discussing these, but espoused the position
that under the circumstances it was better than nothing and
that, anyway, homosexuality was "just another sexual op-
tion." He longed for a "female lover," but his passivity
prevented him from making active efforts to find one. He
usually wanted girls to call him and offer themselves and
felt hurt when they didn't. Despite his role as a "sexual
adventurer" (Sorensen 1973), he balked at accepting the
overtures of the 14- and 15-year-olds he met at parties and

who made their availability evident to him. He was regularly anxious lest he be impotent, though in fact he never was; he experienced the girls with whom he was involved as sexually demanding and felt sure that when they didn't call him it was because they found him sexually inadequate or inept.

Jonathan thus exemplified many aspects of the situation of the male adolescent caught up in the "new sexuality." He conformed to the traditional stance of the young male adventurer, but his developmentally determined passivity led him to accept with relief—even to value—the new active stance of the "liberated" young women in his peer group. At the same time, their very aggressiveness and explicitness threatened him with what Ginsberg, Frosch, and Shapiro (1972) have called "the new impotence" and intensified his tendencies to passive avoidance.

The concern of young men regarding their sexual performance and their tendency to measure their self-esteem thereby is no new phenomenon. It does appear, however, to have been intensified by the increasingly explicit demands of younger women for sexual satisfaction and by their new emphasis on orgasm—even multiple orgasm—as the expected outcome of all sexual acts. Unfortunately, some of those young women who do not readily "achieve" this goal experience the same performance anxiety as do their male counterparts. Nancy, just 20, had been having intercourse since 17 in a succession of "serially monogamous" relationships. That she never experienced orgasm in intercourse was a source of great shame to her and left her feeling inadequate and defective. Pleasure she had felt, but this did not measure up to her expectations. It did not occur to her that questions of technique and timing might be involved, although she was able to achieve orgasm easily with masturbation. In her view, she was "frigid" and thus deeply inferior.

The current permissive tendencies regarding homosexuality tended to soften the definition of Jonathan's sexual preference.* He felt no great pressure to suppress or repress his homosexual wishes, secure in the knowledge that, at least in the milieu in which he lived, no intense stigma would be attached to them. Indeed, he even gave some passing consideration to joining the Gay Liberation group in his university despite his conviction that he was basically heterosexual, as indeed he was. His position was thus akin to that of many of Peplau's female subjects—tolerant toward and even attracted to a bisexual identity because it promised an easier, less tension-laden solution than a rigorously heterosexual one.

Mary and Jonathan have, in their own way, adapted to the multiple demands of adolescence and the "new sexuality." For a significant number of young people, however, these demands are overwhelming and unmanageable. In this, of course, there is nothing intrinsically new; the sexual pressures of adolescence have always posed a threat to some, who have taken refuge from them in a variety of psychological positions and institutional settings, such as the monastic and conventual ones provided by traditional religious bodies and postures of ascetics and instinctual renunciation of the kind referred to by Anna Freud (1958). The decline of conventional organized religion and of its appeal to young

---

* This preceded, of course, the outbreak of the AIDS epidemic (v.i.).

people has led inevitably to the emergence of alternative institutions that offer the vulnerable the same sort of haven. In the past three decades a host of new or exotic religious groups have appeared on the American scene, each characterized by, among other things, a puritanical code of morality that sets firm limits to permissible sexual behavior (cf. Johnson 1975). The Hare Krishna group, for instance, limits sexual activity within marriage to purposes of reproduction and prohibits any sexual congress among its adherents after the age of 30. Fundamentalist Christian groups assert the validity of traditional constraints on premarital sexuality and on the sanctity of virginity and the pure life. Clearly, to adolescents who find themselves troubled by the new permissiveness and the onslaught of media-born sexual stimulation, such doctrines provide a welcome relief.

The sexual revolution, therefore, whatever its impact upon the adult population, has introduced nothing truly new to the adolescent world. Sexual experimentation, intense sexual passion, endless sexual curiosity, and the longing and search for suitable sexual partners have always been a part of the adolescent experience. What the new morality has done is reduce the strength of old constraints and inhibitions so that at least among middle class adolescents (and increasingly among working class youth as well), a relatively guilt-free flowering of manifest sexual experience is occurring earlier than it did a generation ago. Fears of the adult world to the contrary notwithstanding, there is no evidence that sexual promiscuity or rampant perverse sexual behavior has been the consequence of this loosening of old restraints. I know of no evidence, for instance, of increases in sadomasochistic or other perverse practices among young people, despite the proliferation of pornographic representations and explicit advertisements in the "personal" columns of literary publications. Our heightened concern about sexual abuse of children—usually intrafamilial—seems to reflect less an increased occurrence than an enhanced awareness, itself facilitated by greater openness about sexual behavior of all kinds. Certainly there is no evidence that the most fundamental taboo—that on mother-son incest—has been breached. Indeed, the greater ease of accessibility of exogamous sexual partners tends in all probability to reduce the temptations to incestuous alliances, particularly the brother-sister incest so often portrayed in romantic literature.

Anna Freud (Shengold and McLaughlin 1976) acknowledged that in contemporary adolescents the battle against incest and incestuous fantasies goes on as before, with the same defenses and with no less success. In her view, however, the "free" sexual behavior of contemporary youth and their sexual exhibitionism reflect the cessation of the old battle against pregenital sexuality and are used in many cases as a way of punishing the parents who still adhere to traditional standards of conduct. Although this tendentious, conflict-related "use" of "the new sexuality" doubtless applies in some cases, the formulation seems to me an illustration of the kind of overgeneralization from the clinical situation against which Offer has warned us. Sorensen's modal adolescents did not report serious conflict with their parents about their sexual behavior. Chess, Thomas, and Cameron similarly found a kind of tacit acceptance by parents of their children's sexual activity, in some cases out of resignation, no doubt, but seldom with the sense of being "punished":

Adolescence and "The New Sexuality"

There was . . . little intergenerational discussion of actual sexual behavior [except as] a result of conflict regarding the adolescent's behavior. The parents had a general idea of the extent of their youngsters' sexual activity, and in most cases their assumptions appeared correct. . . . By the time these youngsters were sixteen, sex was a closed topic between themselves and their parents. The adolescents guarded their privacy carefully, and for the most part parents respected that privacy . . . parents did not attempt to impose their own ethical values on their children. . . . Most of the youngsters and parents were fairly open and comfortable, however, when talking about sex to . . . interviewers . . . the avoidance of sex discussions by parents and youngsters is a manifestation of the adolescent's drive to establish independence and *a way of avoiding the family tensions and conflicts that such discussions might produce.* (1976:695–699; my italics)

It seems, then, that what has emerged is a new pattern of sexual involvement characterized by premarital monogamous attachments that are maintained with relative fidelity "as long as we dig each other," i.e., Sorensen's (1973) pattern of "serial monogamy." There is no evidence that this greater sexual freedom has interfered in any significant way with the adaptive success of most of this generation's adolescents. Consistent with the new emphasis on self-realization and career development for girls, however, it does appear that this generation's adolescents look forward with less interest to ultimate marriage and with considerably less anticipation, or at least deferral of, ultimate childbearing as a longtime life goal.

What we have described can scarcely be called a sexual revolution at all. It seems, rather, to be an evolutionary change in the cultural pattern of sexual mores and values with which most adolescents are comfortable. For some, the new freedom does arouse anxiety, especially in relation to sexual performance, generally transitory but occasionally imbricated with a neurotic pattern of inhibition and avoidance. For those even more threatened by the lack of structure and definition in the current sexual atmosphere, however, and who require social and ideological support for maintaining a more restrained approach to sexuality, new institutions have arisen to replace some of the old ones that are no longer effective—old wine in new bottles, perhaps. Only those on the most vulnerable edge of the spectrum of personality development require, as they always have, the ultimate redress of personality disintegration and ego regression as the last resort in coping with the stresses engendered by the "new sexuality."

## AIDS and the "New Sexuality"

The appearance, at the beginning of the 1980s, of a new and lethal sexual scourge in the form of Acquired Immune Deficiency Syndrome (AIDS) has, in certain circles at least, effected major changes in sexual behavior. Among many male homosexuals, in particular, heedless promiscuity has been replaced by "safe" sexual practices, even celibacy. The continuing spread of the disease is now limited largely to intravenous drug abusers and their sexual partners, who are relatively uninfluenced by educational and informational campaigns.

What, if anything, has been the impact of this plague on adolescent sexual behavior? Remarkably, at least at the time of writing (May 1989), very little research bearing on this question has been published. Concern about the potential spread of AIDS in this sexually active (and therefore potentially vulnerable) population has led to extensive discussion of educational programs and techniques, particularly in view of the fact that "fully one fourth of all sexually active adolescents will become infected with a sexually transmitted disease before graduating from high school, a grave situation that makes AIDS a potential time bomb for millions of American youth" (Carnegie Council 1989:25). Enthusiasm for such efforts is, however, tempered by the knowledge that earlier sex education programs addressed to adolescents have shown little evidence of success. This has tended to frustrate the efforts of adults to limit or control adolescents' sexual behavior — especially in a cultural context in which increasingly unambiguous sexual stimulation is constantly purveyed by the entertainment media.

In a recent study, DiClemente, Boyer, and Morales showed that "Black and Latino adolescents" in San Francisco "were approximately twice as likely as White adolescents to have misconceptions about the causal transmission of AIDS" (1988:55). While the minority-group adolescents had more misconceptions about the causes and transmission of the disease, far fewer of them knew that the use of condoms during intercourse would lower the risk of transmission. Chandarana (1989) noted that an educational program increased the knowledge about AIDS in a group of seventh and eighth graders, but there is no indication of any effect on actual sex practices, since these children are below the usual age of sexual activity. In point of fact, Kirby et al. (1989) found that although a large percentage of adolescent boys who received a mailing about condoms and their use read the material and sent for a free supply, no differences could later be found between these young males and a control group in attitudes toward condom use or in actual sexual practices.

Thus it appears from currently available data that the AIDS epidemic has had little or at least marginal effect on adolescent sexual conduct. It seems likely that cognitive awareness may be outdone by the pressure of impulse, coupled with the adolescent's characteristic sense of omnipotence and invulnerability ("it can't happen to me"). It may be that more time, more profound penetration of new social constraints, and less ambiguity in transmitted information will be needed before a substantial change occurs in the sexual mores of American adolescents.

## Adolescent Pregnancy

Similar considerations apply to the major social problem of adolescent pregnancy. The ubiquitous sexual pressures attending and consequent on pubertal development ensure that sexual intercourse will ensue in a sizable proportion of adolescents; the "new morality" described earlier defines a trend toward its occurrence earlier and more frequently than was the case in Western culture a generation ago. Inevitably, some proportion of these sexual encounters will result in pregnancies.

Strikingly, however, there exists a wide discrepancy between the incidence of adolescent pregnancies in the United States and that in other industrialized countries. In 1981 the adolescent pregnancy rate (15–19-year-olds) in the United States was 96:1000, compared with 14:1000 in the Netherlands. Even excluding blacks, among whom the rate is particularly high, the U.S. rate for white adolescents was 83:1000

(McAnarney and Hendee 1989:74). Evidently, strong cultural forces are at work to account for so massive a difference.

A major factor is, of course, the difference in attitudes toward and use of contraceptives. The moralism that pervades American culture generates a high level of shame and discomfort among young people in this regard; to use contraceptive devices implies that sex is planned and anticipated, rather than being "natural" and the product of "irresistible impulse." Many adults, especially those associated with orthodox and fundamentalist religious groups, appalled by the "immorality" they perceive as the source of adolescent pregnancies, simultaneously inveigh against open discussion or education about contraceptives (not to mention their easy availability) as contrary to their religious convictions or as encouragements to such "immorality." Where "the message to avoid unwanted pregnancies is strong and clear in the Scandinavian countries, for example, it is not nearly so clear in the United States" (McAnarney and Hendee 1989:74). Further, to many American adolescent males, particularly in certain ethnic subgroups, the capacity to impregnate is a mark of virility, reducing any incentive to employ contraceptive devices. In general, adolescents who lack social and family support are more likely to engage in sexual intercourse early and thus place themselves at risk for pregnancy. In a culture in which single parent families are increasingly the rule—particularly in the "culture of poverty"—and where many children and adolescents are inclined to use sexuality as a means of obtaining the illusion of longed-for nurturance and intimacy, such outcomes are all too frequently preordained.

Unfortunately, as noted earlier, there is little evidence

that formal (school-based) sex education has any significant effect on adolescent sexual behavior, certainly none that indicates any tendency toward more enlightened use of contraception. School-based clinics offering sexual counseling and family planning services have been shown to be of value, but in many American communities these have been opposed by parents who see them as "condoning" or "promoting" sexual license.

In the face of the glamorization of sex in the media, such attitudes, reflecting the moralistic hypocrisy that characterizes much of the American attitude about sexuality in general, serve merely to drive adolescent sexuality underground (since it cannot be stopped). They thus discourage appropriate use of contraceptive and prenatal services and accentuate the very problem they propose to avert.

The consequences of this conflict between nature and culture are (1) that about 40 percent of adolescent pregnancies are terminated by induced abortions (a number unlikely to be reduced by recent Supreme Court decisions) and (2) massive interference with normal adolescent development for many of those girls who carry their pregnancies to term and who, in conformity with recent attitudinal shifts, elect to keep their babies rather than place them for adoption. Education is aborted or delayed, career possibilities frustrated, and assumption of adult autonomy interfered with, and repeated pregnancies and social dependency are frequent outcomes. It is these cases that are the true casualties of "the new sexuality."

# 5

# The Adolescent as Shaper and as Barometer of Culture

Today's adolescents are, as noted, on the front lines of cultural change. In that position they are not only vulnerable to the impact of socioeconomic and cultural perturbations; they also serve as messengers to those behind the lines who more or less eagerly await the latest dispatches from the front.

It has not been difficult to demonstrate in the previous chapters the former of these processes. The latter is, however, less easy to delineate. Particularly is this true because the very definition of adolescents as a group with possible agency is, in historical perspective, quite recent; further, in much of the world the pace of cultural change has, at least until the post–World War II era, been slow indeed. Thus adolescents have emerged as instruments of cultural change largely in the past four decades in developed and developing societies whose histories are still being written or will not be written for some time to come.

## Adolescents as Instruments

None have been more aware of the potentiality of youth as agents of cultural transformation than the leaders of the totalitarian regimes of the twentieth century. Nazi German's Hitler Youth, the Soviet Komsomol, and Mao Tsetung's Red Guard all represent efforts—generally successful ones—to harness the energy, activism, and ideological fervor of adolescents to the cause of revolutionary social change.

Erikson has, in a series of studies (1964, 1968), detailed the appeal of ideology for adolescents. He refers to the "totalistic" quality of their thinking, the narcissistic satisfaction derived from the sense of knowing the "truth," the restitutive value, at a time of developmental flux and of revision of attitudes toward relations with the adult world, of a firm and categorical system of beliefs that knows no doubts, admits no uncertainty. "The adolescent," he states, "learns to grasp the flux of time, to anticipate the future in a coherent way, to perceive ideas and to assert ideals, to take—in short—an *ideological* position for which the younger child is cognitively not prepared" (1968:225). "Where historical and technological development . . . severely encroach upon deeply rooted or strongly emerging identities (i.e., agrarian, feudal, patrician) on a large scale, youth feels endangered, individually and collectively, whereupon it becomes ready to support doctrines offering a total immersion in a synthetic identity (extreme nationalism, racism or class consciousness) and a collective condemnation of a totally stereotyped enemy of the new identity" (ibid.: 89).

It was in just such a historical context, Erikson points out, that Hitler "established an organization, a training, and a motto which would direct all adolescent energy into National Socialism. The organization was the Hitler Youth; the motto, 'Youth shapes its own destiny' " (ibid.: 309). It was in a similar context that Mao Tse-tung enlisted Chinese adolescents in the service of his Cultural Revolution, creating the Red Guard, which served as the primary enforcers of doctrinal purity and "proletarian consciousness." Those who lived through the Cultural Revolution can recount endless tales of the violence, brutality, and mindless destructiveness of adolescents fired by ideological fervor and unrestrained by such ancient Chinese values as veneration for the aged and the scholar and respect for traditional culture and its artifacts. Leys reports the account of a "university graduate" who told him "how schoolboys forced old men to kneel on shards, and how, on another occasion, boys with bayonets stabbed the corpses of rebels strung up on lampposts along the street in Quangchow. . . . No one, he adds, dared say or do anything or interfere in any way for fear of being accused of 'bourgeois humanism' or of culpable compassion for the class enemy" (1979:141). Thus, at least during the ascendancy of their adult mentors, these young people exerted a powerful influence on the culture in which they lived. By projecting their own (now tenuous) fantasies of infantile omnipotence onto their charismatic leaders, the youthful totalitarians could recapture, by means of identification, a sense of unlimited power and unchallengeable authority.

[ 87 ]

In China at least the effects of Red Guard terror are still in evidence; in Leys' words, "the children of the cultural revolution are savage orphans who when their adventure was over destroyed the tribal totem (i.e., Mao)" (ibid.: 109). Anthony Burgess' *A Clockwork Orange* presents a fictional version of such a situation, in which a society is dominated and terrorized by a youth culture operating in the service of a futuristic British regime strongly resembling, in its language and social control processes, Stalin's Soviet Union or the nightmare state of Zamyatin's *We* or Orwell's *1984*.

During a period in which the young thugs of the Red Guard and the Khmer Rouge were laying seige to their cultures in the service of their new masters, some older adolescents and youths in the industrialized world were engaged in what, at least at the time, appeared to be a serious revolt against the established leaders of their societies. In the United States, in France, in Germany, in Japan, and elsewhere, groups of students and in some cases pseudostudents rose against both the educational and political institutions, demanding "reforms" and a greater voice in the formation and execution of official policies. To many of the participants, and to some of the bemused adults that observed them, this revolt contained the seeds of a true revolution, one that sought to create a new society with new cultural forms and institutions. It seemed, that is, that while Mao's and Pol Pot's youths were acting in the service of an existent revolution the youth of the developed countries were seeking to create one of their own.

Now, two decades later, it is clear that no revolution occurred, nor did the basic structure of the society or its institutions undergo much in the way of fundamental change. And yet important consequences did emerge from the youth powered upheavals of the sixties and seventies. The civil rights of minority groups in the United States were measurably strengthened and legislatively reinforced; the Vietnam War was brought to its inglorious close. In both cases the political leadership of the movements was, as would be expected, in the hands of adults, but the manpower, the fervor, the relentless pressure of ardent numbers, and the dedicated commitment to the ultimate goal came from the ranks of adolescents and that even newer social grouping, "youth" (Keniston 1971). Illustrative of the value of such ideological commitment to the individual adolescent is the case of an extraordinarily bright and gifted 15-year-old girl, the product of an enormously complex family of mixed racial origin and radical political orientation, who came to treatment in the throes of a moderately severe depression that was significantly interfering with her academic and social life. Consistent with her family background, she was deeply interested in the antinuclear movement and spent a considerable amount of time in treatment talking about her involvement with various aspects of the then current campaign against the development of nuclear reactors. She proceeded quite well in therapy, however, and was deeply engaged in examining her feelings about her relations with her parents and her profound sense of disappointment and disillusionment in them. When the Three Mile Island incident occurred, this girl was galvanized into activity. She became energized by the activation of the movement around this near-disaster and profoundly immersed herself in the series of demonstrations, marches, and protests that came in its wake. Her depression lifted, and it became clear that she had no time in her busy schedule for the luxury of psychotherapy. She thanked me for my help and made it clear that life was now offering her more in terms of purpose and fulfillment than I was able to give her. That, in sum, was the end of her psychotherapy.

In the aftermath of those passionate years, the culture is vastly different from what it had been before the 1960s. New styles, new folkways introduced by the young, have come to pervade the society and have spread downward to the children and upward toward the adult world. Indeed, many of the new mores introduced by the young and the rebellious have been co-opted by the most conservative elements in the culture; the blue denim and long hair that emerged on the college campuses of the 1960s have become the uniform of the construction workers and teamsters of the 1980s. Brake points that "punk" clothing "began by using the most rejected and contemptible clothing basis — garbage bags. But punk attire moved up-market as Zandra Rhodes used it as a fashion theme" (1985:72). The single earring worn in the right ear adopted as a sign by the homosexual men of the 1970s became the ubiquitous accessory of the British working class adolescent in the eighties, although it is worn in the left ear or both ears. It appears that this fashion initially represented a statement of negation — "I am not a homosexual, and I show my badge to prove it." By now, however, it is simply seen "as what's done" (M. Laufer, personal communication) with its original rationale, like that of many culturally and subculturally syntonic behaviors, repressed or denied.

In a recent news dispatch Williams (1988) reports and implicitly deplores the current American fashion for violent, obscene, and abusive language, displayed both in films and television and in general social discourse. She quotes the psychoanalyst Willard Gaylin, who said, correctly, "The deterioration of politeness and public manner is at a sufficiently rapid stage to be measurable within any one individual's experience." Blame for this turn has been laid by some at the feet of Freud, to whose discovery of the role of repression in the generation of neurosis is ascribed the popular misconception that the uninhibited expression of "feelings" is salubrious. Although it is true that "traditional" (i.e., Victorian) standards of propriety began to crumble during the "jazz age" of the 1920s, it was most particularly during the 1960s, in the context of the social turbulence accompanying the civil rights movement and the anti–Vietnam War demonstrations, that the barriers that maintain civility and social discourse truly crumbled away. Student protesters chanting, "Off the pigs," set the tone for the increasing acceptance of expressions of naked violence in public utterance; at the same time overt sexual appeal (as opposed to innuendo) began to appear in music and lyrics addressed by youthful performers to younger audiences.*

The loosening of standards of civility pervades the culture, of course, and cannot be ascribed entirely to the influence of adolescents and youth. They are as much the patient as the agent of the social changes that have induced this process. Among these the simultaneous emergence of the women's liberation movement, spearheaded by young women of college and graduate school age under the tutelage of their older "sisters," has intensified the pervasive spread of uninhibited speech, giving women the "right" to use freely

---

* The modes of language and behavior of the Vietnam War protesters have parallels with those of the English football louts (e.g., urinating on policemen); both exemplify the regressive potential inherent in groups of angry, alienated, and disaffected young people whose individual superegos are ceded to the group itself (cf. Freud 1921) or are dissolved in alcohol or marijuana.

words and phraseology (chiefly scatological) formerly reserved, at least in public, to men. Thus a recent 18-year-old
college freshman (freshwoman?) patient of impeccable upper middle class background habitually expressed herself
quite matter-of-factly, unselfconsciously, and with no sense
either of exhibitionism or shame in language that would, a
generation ago, have made a stevedore blush.

It may be fruitless to pursue the question of priority in
this matter; whether, for instance, the pervasiveness of scatological and copulatory idiom in certain adult-made films
is a stimulus and a model for the language patterns of their
largely adolescent audiences or whether the filmmakers are
simply responding to preexisting changes in the standards
of verbal usage among the members of their intended market is probably undeterminable at this time. In all likeli-
hood it is a spiraling process of mutual influence that continues to propel movie dialogue to newer heights of vulgarity
or, if one will, openness. Similar questions may arise regarding popular music performances, where the harmlessly
screaming teenage girls of the thirties and forties contrast
sharply with the violent, at times murderous, throngs of
male and female adolescents at the rock concerts of the
seventies and eighties. To what degree, that is, this difference is the result of the manipulative tactics of adult pro-
moters, publicists, and drug peddlers and to what extent it
represents an autonomous change in adolescent behavior
patterns and demographic characteristics is beyond determination. In either case, the current ritual pattern of high-
decibel performance, marijuana and alcohol indulgence, and
postconcert violence has come to affect Western culture in
a number of ways, not least in the demand it creates for

police protection and other community services.* Recent developments in the USSR suggest that similar trends may be in the process of occurring there as well.

Spitz (1987) and others have called attention to a notable contribution of adolescents to the urban culture, the phenomenon of "graffiti" art. Graffiti have an ancient history, as any visitor to ancient or classical monuments in the Old World can attest. But their emergence as an intrusive, inescapable part of the urban scene—particularly, their flamboyant presence on the walls of subway cars of major cities —has been a product of contemporary American culture. These spray-painted images have been, almost exclusively, the work adolescent males, generally of minority group background. Ambivalently received by the general public, they rapidly became symbolic statements of the conflict between the "establishment," which sought endlessly to eradicate them and to punish those who "perpetrated" them, and the angry underclass youths who found in this art form a means of expressing their rage and declaring their individual and collective identities.

In the early 1980s a short-lived effort was made by the art establishment to embrace this popular medium. Some enterprising collectors and avant-garde galleries began to purchase and exhibit works of graffiti artists; works made, however, self-consciously on canvas or panels rather than spontaneously in public places. In this way graffiti sought to assert a significant role in middle-class culture. In the end only one graffiti artist, the late Jean-Michel Basquiat,

* A recent Supreme Court decision affirmed the right of municipal authorities to impose regulatory restraint on the volume level of such performances.

succeeded in crossing the divide and achieving success in the "official" art world. More recently the New York subway system has claimed success in its efforts to eliminate graffiti from its cars, and the successors to the graffiti painters appear to have moved on to more destructive modes of delinquency. But a recent visitor to Paris has noted that the cars in the Metro are now covered with spray-painted "tags"; it appears that New York may have succeeded not in eradicating graffiti but merely in exporting them.

The reflections in this and previous chapters serve, I believe, to support the thesis that adolescence is a—perhaps the—barometer of culture. Its very transitional status illuminates the particular characteristics of the stages that precede and follow it—childhood and adulthood—and the process and meaning of passage from the one to the other. As Werner put it:

> Adolescence in the primitive society means the period of preparation for entrance into an immutable social sphere. The young man after an initiation becomes an actual part of the past of the tribe, since the life of the community consists in the preservation and continuation of its eternal patterns. Adolescence in the advanced cultural forms, however, may mean all this and something more. It may mean preparation for a new pattern of life, for an ever changing future. . . . (1948:27)

Every culture evolves a system of child rearing practices designed, consciously or unconsciously, to produce the kind of adults that it needs and values. Certain basic biologically determined aspects of human nature are, in Melford Spiro's (1987) words, "pan-human"; it is in the interplay between these human universals and the particularities of familial and cultural variability that personalities are formed, traditions are transmitted, and, where desired, innovations are introduced. Much of this process goes on, of course, in early childhood; indeed, by the time the child reaches puberty he or she has already been indoctrinated with major elements of cultural lore. This is, after all, what education—formal or informal—is all about. In "primitive" cultures the father teaches his young son to use a spear and to bait fishhooks; the mother teaches her little daughter to plants yams and weave raffia cloth. In industrialized cultures the teacher demonstrates the use of calculators and children of both sexes gather around the computer terminal.

Still it is adolescence—or its analogues—that, as Erikson showed, puts the definitive cultural stamp on the evolving character and that serves as the weathervane to the observer of the cultural climate. The Nandi girl's silent, stoic submission to the excision of her clitoris epitomizes the role she as a woman will play in a highly patriarchal culture; in contrast, the American Jewish girl's celebration of the bas mitzvah ceremony (a recent noncanonical innovation) betokens the increasing equalization of gender roles in middle class Western societies. Nothing can be a more telling indicator of America's transformation from a producing to a consuming society than the sharp decline in membership in 4-H Clubs over the past generation. These teenage agricultural associates, once the proud symbol of the American farming community, have dwindled from 95,674 in 1972 to 77,643 in 1988; the number of youths enrolled declined from 2,173,799 to 1,574,872 in the same period.[*]

[*] Data provided by U.S. Department of Agriculture Extension Service.

Granted the post–baby boom drop in the adolescent population, this still represents a profound shift in the location and the vocational commitment of American youth.

As large scale mechanized commercial agriculture replaces the family farm all over the industrialized world, more and more once rural families—including their adolescent children—are being swept into the expanding urban culture, with all its benefits and its disadvantages. For, as we have seen earlier, it is urbanization above all that creates the conditions that define adolescence as we know it, that demarcates industrial and postindustrial societies from the traditional ones. It is precisely the character of adolescent life, the definition of an institutionalized adolescent stage, that most sharply distinguishes these cultural forms.

In *The Satanic Verses*, Rushdie (1988) depicts with hallucinatory clarity and mordant wit the adaptation of an immigrant Bangladeshi family—and, in particular, of their adolescent daughters—to the alien mores and institutions of present day London. Unlike the compliant, unaggressive, traditional adolescents described by Sinha (1965), these girls are swept up in the freewheeling, verbally explicit, rebellious, and sexually uninhibited behaviors that have characterized Western urban—and particularly British—working and lower middle class youth in the latter half of the twentieth century. "Bangladesh," says one, "in't nothing to me. Just some place Dad and Mum keep banging on about" (Rushdie 1988:259), while their mother complains, "It seems everything I used to know is a lie, such as the idea that young girls should help their mothers, think of marriage, attend to studies" (ibid.: 276).

Coincidentally, in a BBC TV talk show at about the time of the novel's publication nature imitated art: an immigrant

Indian mother bemoaned the impact of London life on her adolescent daughters—in particular, on their relations with boys—and, to the dismay of her more acculturated husband, announced her firm intention to take them back to their native soil so that they could grow up as proper Indian girls should. This implied not only submission to traditional conventions but specifically their acceptance of arranged marriages. The clash of cultures thus finds its most intense and strident expression in the conflict around the behavior of adolescents. It is in such situations that the concept of the "generation gap" takes on genuine meaning. Rushdie's adolescents, with their bare midriffs, their disdain for formal learning, their spiked and multicolored hairdos, and their blatant sexuality, throw into sharp relief the values of the mass culture into which they are assimilating and into which, willy-nilly, their parents are being reluctantly drawn.

We began this survey with a casual impression of homogeneity. We end it with a sense of diversity, a diversity based on differences in social class, cultural tradition, and socioeconomic development. It is clear that any formulation of the psychology of "normal" adolescence that suggests pan-human uniformity or biologically based universality is open to serious doubt. Puberty is, of course, a human universal. But adolescence—becoming adult—is more than the adaptation to puberty. It is molded by the very nature of adulthood as that varies from culture to culture, by the ecological and economic realities that characterize each society, and by the sanctions and prohibitions that each society imposes on drive expression and the possibilities for self-realization. The transition from the status of child to that of adult may be brief or protracted; it may be marked by defined rituals or by indefinite and conflicting social markers; it may require unquestioning adherence to traditional role behaviors or encourage open, exploratory pursuit of goals self-chosen through complex processes of "identity formation."

It would be foolish to define Western adolescence in terms of the fads and fashions that come and go from year to year, from place to place. "Rebelliousness," "conformity," long hair, short hair, political commitment, political apathy — these shift and fluctuate like skirt lengths, according to the state of the economy and the vagaries of intercurrent events. What demarcates adolescence in industrialized societies is precisely this lack of definition, this openness to change, this susceptibility to the influence of political and technological developments. It is just this openness that is the despair of the elders, who wish to see their children's adolescence as an enactment of the retrospectively distorted memory of their own and who are eternally discomfited by the cultural changes of which their adolescent offspring are the barometers. But such intergenerational continuity can occur only in the rapidly disappearing isolation of the desert or the rain forest. As the gerontocracy of the People's Republic of China is coming to see, one cannot have the benefits of industrialization and international communication without the price of cultural transformation and it is the students—the adolescents and "youth"—who carry the banners that mark such inexorable change.

For the student of adolescence the implications are equally clear: An exclusive focus on intrapsychic conflict and the vagaries of the Oedipus complex (positive and negative) will provide only a constricted view of the broad and rich terrain in which the adolescent lives. As Shapiro (1985) has pointed out, some ability to remain *au courant* with the rapidly shifting patterns of adolescent speech (themselves largely media-shaped) is a necessary, if not sufficient, requirement for effective dialogue. And, as innumerable cultural anthropologists have demonstrated, a grasp of prevailing folkways is indispensible for assigning meaning to any behavioral datum in any culture, including the culture of adolescence. Thus, as cultures become more complex and variegated, the study of adolescence will increasingly require interdisciplinary collaboration in which the psychoanalyst will play an essential, if not a pre-eminent, role. Psychoanalysis has in the past century made invaluable contributions to our understanding of both normal and pathological development in adolescence. Its future lies, I believe, in its ability to integrate its unique vision with those of its peers in the human sciences, and its willingness, at last, to assume its full and proper membership in the academic community.

# REFERENCES

Adelson, J. 1975. The development of ideology in adolescence. In S. Dragastin and G. Elder, eds., *Adolescence in the Life Cycle*, pp. 63–78. New York: Wiley.

Andrews, A. 1967. *The Greeks*. London: Hutchinson.

Anthony, E. J. 1969. The reactions of adults to adolescents and their behavior. In A. Esman, ed., *The Psychology of Adolescence*, pp. 467–494. New York: International Universities Press.

Aries, P. 1962. *Centuries of Childhood*. New York: Knopf.

Arlow, J. 1951. A psychoanalytic study of a religious initiation rite: Bar Mitzvah. *Psychoanalytic Study of the Child*, 6:353–374. New York: International Universities Press.

Barglow, P., and M. Schaefer. 1979. The fate of the feminine self—normative adolescent regression. In M. Sugar, ed., *Female Adolescent Development*, pp. 201–213. New York: Brunner/Mazel.

# References

Baumrind, D. 1975. Early socialization and adolescent compe-
tence. In S. Dragastin and G. Elder, eds., *Adolescence in the
Life Cycle*, pp. 117–143. New York: Wiley.

Bell, D. 1978. *The Cultural Contradictions of Capitalism*, 2d ed.
London: Heinemann.

Blos, P. 1961. Preoedipal factors in the etiology of female delinquency. *Psychoanalytic Study of the Child*, 12:229–249. New
York: International Universities Press.

Blos, P. 1962. *On Adolescence—A Psychoanalytic Interpretation*.
New York: Free Press of Glencoe.

Blos, P. 1971. The generation gap—fact or fiction? *Adolescent
Psychiatry*, 1:5–13.

Brake, M. 1985. *Comparative Youth Culture*. London and New
York: Routledge and Kegan Paul.

Burgess, A. 1962. *A Clockwork Orange*. New York: Norton.

Carnegie Council on Adolescent Development. 1989. *Turning
Points: Preparing American Youth for the 21st Century*. New
York: Carnegie Corporation of New York.

Chandarana, P. 1989. AIDS programs in schools successful at edu-
cating, student's perceptions. Cited in *Psychiatric News* (April),
21:8.

Chess, S., A. Thomas, and M. Cameron. 1976. Sexual attitudes and
behavior patterns in a middle class adolescent population. *Amer.
J. Orthopsychiatry*, 46:689–701.

Clarke, J., S. Hill, T. Jefferson, and B. Roberts. 1975. Subcultures,
cultures and class. In S. Hill & T. Jefferson, eds., *Resistance
Through Rituals: Youth Subcultures in Post-war Britain*, pp. 9–
74. London: Hutchinson.

Coleman, J. 1961. *The Adolescent Society*. Glencoe: Free Press.

Coleman, J., and T. Hüsen. 1985. *Becoming Adult in a Changing
Society*. Paris: OECD.

Csikszentmihalyi, M., and R. Lanson. 1984. *Being Adolescent:
Conflict and Growth in the Teen-age Years*. New York: Basic
Books.

Delors, J. 1977. The attitudes of adolescents to education and
work. In J. Hill & F. Mönks, eds. *Adolescence and Youth in*

# References

*Prospect*, pp. 201–212. Guildford: IPC Science & Technology Press.

DiClemente, R., C. Boyer, and E. Morales. 1988. Minorities and AIDS: Knowledge, attitudes and misconceptions among Black and Latino adolescents. *Amer. J. Public Health*, 78:55–57.

Douvan, E., and J. Adelson. 1966. *The Adolescent Experience*. New York: Wiley.

Dulit, E. 1972. Adolescent thinking à la Piaget: The formal stage. *J. Youth and Adolescence*, 1:281–301.

Erikson, E. 1950. *Childhood and Society*. New York: Norton.

Erikson, E. 1964. *Insight and Responsibility*. New York: Norton.

Erikson, E. 1968. *Identity, Youth, and Crisis*. New York: Norton.

Erikson, E. 1975. Reflections on the revolt of humanist youth. In *Life History and the Historical Moment*, pp. 193–224. New York: Norton.

Esman, A. 1972. Adolescence and the consolidation of values. In S. C. Post, ed., *Moral Values and the Superego Concept in Psychoanalysis*, pp. 87–100. New York: International Universities Press.

Esman, A. 1977. Changing values: Their implications for adolescent development and psychoanalytic ideas. *Adolescent Psychiatry*, 5:18–34.

Esman, A. 1982. Fathers and adolescent sons. In S. Cath, A. Gurwitt, and J. Ross, eds., *Father and Child: Developmental and Clinical Perspectives*, pp. 265–274. Boston: Little, Brown.

Freeman, D. 1983. *The Making and Unmaking of an Anthropological Myth*. Cambridge: Harvard University Press.

Freud, A. 1958. Adolescence. *Psychoanalytic Study of the Child*, 13:255–278. New York: International Universities Press.

Freud, A. 1969. Adolescence as a developmental disturbance. *The Writings of Anna Freud*, 7:39–47. New York: International Universities Press, 1971.

Freud, S. *Standard Edition of the Complete Psychological Works of Sigmund Freud*. James Strachey, tr. and ed. 24 vols. London: Hogarth Press, 1953–1974. Hereafter cited as *S.E.*

Freud, S. 1895. On the grounds for detaching a particular syndrome from neuraesthenia under the description "anxiety neurosis." *S.E.* 3:90–115.

Freud, S. 1905. The transformations of puberty. *(Three Essays on the Theory of Sexuality.)* S.E., 7:207–243.

Freud, S. 1921. *Group Psychology and the Analysis of the Ego.* S.E., 18:69–145.

Freud, S. 1930. *Civilization and Its Discontents. S.E.,* 21:64–145.

Freud, S. 1954. *The Origins of Psychoanalysis.* M. Bonaparte, A. Freud, and E. Kris., eds. New York: Basic Books.

Friedenberg, E. 1959. *The Vanishing Adolescent.* New York: Dell.

Frith, S., and H. Horne. 1981. *Art into Pop.* London: Methuen.

Gadpaille, W. 1977. Adolescence: Developmental stage or cultural artifact? *Adolescent Psychiatry,* 5:143–150.

GAP (Group for the Advancement of Psychiatry). 1968. *Normal Adolescence.* New York: GAP.

Gillis, J. 1973. Conformity and rebellion. *Hist. of Education Quarterly,* 13:249–260.

Ginsberg, G., W. Frosch, and T. Shapiro. 1972. The new impotence. *Arch. Gen. Psychiatry,* 26:218–220.

Glassner, B., and J. Laughlin. 1987. *Drugs in Adolescent Worlds.* London: Macmillan.

Gottlieb, D., J. Reeves, and W. Ten Houten. 1966. *The Emergence of Youth Societies: A Cross-cultural Approach.* New York: The Free Press.

Gull, W. 1874. Anorexia nervosa (apepsia hysterica, anorexia hysterica). *Trans. of the Clinical Society* (London), 7:22–28.

Hall, G. S. 1904. *Adolescence.* New York: Norton.

Hendin, H. 1975. *Youth in Crisis.* New York: Norton.

Hill, J. and F. Mönks. 1977. *Adolescence & Youth in Prospect.* Guildford: IPC Science & Technology Press.

Hofferth, S., J. Kahn, and W. Baldwin. 1987. Premarital sexual activity among U.S. teenage women over the past three decades. *Family Planning Perspectives* 19:46–53.

Hollingshead, A. 1949/1975. *Elmtown's Youth* and *Elmtown Revisited.* New York: Wiley, 1975.

Jackman, B. and E. Valli. 1988. Children of the dust. *Sunday Times Magazine* (London) November 13:24–31.

# References

Johnson, A. 1975. Drifting on the God circuit. In A. Esman, ed., *The Psychology of Adolescence*, pp. 524–534. New York: International Universities Press.

Joyce, J. 1916. *A Portrait of the Artist as a Young Man.* New York: Viking.

Kandel, D. 1975. Stages in adolescent involvement in drug use. *Science* 190:912–914.

Kandel, D. 1984. Substance abuse by adolescents in Israel and France: a cross-cultural perspective. *Public Health Reports,* 99:277–283.

Kandel, D., and G. Lesser. 1972. *Youth in Two Worlds.* San Francisco: Jossey-Bass.

Kaplan, L. 1984. *Adolescence: The Farewell to Childhood.* New York: Simon & Schuster.

Keniston, K. 1968. *Young Radicals.* New York: Harcourt Brace World.

Keniston, K. 1971. Youth as a stage of life. *Adolescent Psychiatry,* 1:161–175.

Kenyatta, J. (n.d.) *Facing Mount Kenya.* New York: Vintage.

Kett, J. 1977. *Rites of Passage: Adolescence in America, 1790 to the Present.* New York: Basic Books.

Kinsey, A., W. Pomeroy, C. Martin, and P. Gebhard. 1953. *Sexual Behavior in the Human Female.* Philadelphia: Saunders.

Kirby, D., P. Harvey, D. Claussenius, and M. Novar. 1989. A direct mailing to teenage males about condom use: its impact on knowledge, attitudes, and sexual behavior. *Family Planning Perspectives,* 21:12–18.

Kirkpatrick, M. 1989. Society plays significant role in labeling of women as masochistic. *Psychiatric Times* (May):19–21.

Kohlberg, A. 1984. *The Psychology of Moral Development.* San Francisco: Harper & Row.

Kris, E. 1948. Prince Hal's Conflict. *Psychoan. Quarterly,* 7:487–506.

Lacey, W. 1968. *The Family in Classical Greece.* Ithaca: Cornell University Press.

Leys, S. 1979. *Broken Images.* London: Allwin & Busby.

[ 105 ]

References

McAnarney, E. and W. Handee. 1989. Adolescent pregnancy and its consequences. *JAMA* 262:74–77.

McRobbie, A., and J. Garber. 1975. Girls' subcultures. In S. Hill and T. Jefferson, eds., *Resistance through Rituals: Youth Subcultures in Post-war Britain*, pp. 209–22. London: Hutchinson.

Mahler, F. 1977. Adolescent ethics & morals in the year 2000. In Hill and Mönks, op. cit., 79–94.

Mari, J. P. 1988. USA: Les Nouveau Sauvages. *Le Nouvel Observateur* (August 19–25):52–54.

Masterson, J. 1967. The symptomatic adolescent five years later: He didn't grow out of it. *Amer. J. Psychiatry*, 123:1338–1345.

Masterson, J. 1968. The psychiatric significance of adolescent turmoil. In A. Esman, ed., *The Psychology of Adolescence*, pp. 221–228. New York: International Universities Press, 1975.

Mead, M. 1928. *Coming of Age in Samoa*. New York: Morrow.

*Media Book*. 1979. New York: Barlow & Papazian.

Melly, G. 1970. *Revolt into Style: The Pop Arts in Britain*. London: Penguin.

Monarca, S., M. Modolo, V. Stopponi, M. Catanelli, R. Romizi, and L. Santi. 1987. Alcohol, tobacco & psychoactive medicine consumption among high school students of 10 Italian towns. *Int. J. Addictions*, 22:1243–1254.

Morgan, H. 1981. *Drugs in America: A Social History, 1800–1908*. Syracuse: Syracuse University Press.

Mueller, M. 1988. Ces jeunes qui vous fait peur. *Le Nouvel Observateur*, August 19–25:48–51.

Muensterberger, W. 1961. The adolescent in society. In A. Esman, ed., *The Psychology of Adolescence*, pp. 12–44. New York: International Universities Press, 1975.

Offer, D. 1969. *The Psychological World of the Teenager*. New York: Basic Books.

Offer, D., and J. Offer. 1975. *From Teenager to Young Manhood*. New York: Basic Books.

Oldham, D. 1978. Adolescent turmoil: A myth revisited. *Adolescent Psychiatry*, 6:267–282.

Orwell, G. 1949. *1984*. New York: New American Library, 1983.

# References

Peplau, L. 1977. Quoted in *Psychiatric News* (June), 12:32–33.

Piaget, J. 1969. The intellectual development of the adolescent. In A. Esman, ed., *The Psychology of Adolescence*, pp. 104–108. New York: International Universities Press, 1975.

Pirie, P., D. Murray, and R. Luepker. 1988. Smoking preference in a cohort of adolescents, including absentees, dropouts, and transfers. *Am. J. Public Health*, 78:176–178.

Pumeriega, A., P. Edwards, and C. Mitchell. 1984. Anorexia nervosa in black adolescents. *J. Amer. Acad. Child Psychiatry*, 23:111–114.

Rushdie, S. 1988. *The Satanic Verses.* New York: Viking Press.

Schmidt, G., and V. Sigusch. 1972. Changes in sexual behavior among young males and females between 1960–1970. *Arch. Sexual Behavior*, 2:27–45.

Sebald, H. 1984. *Adolescence: A Social Psychological Analysis.* Englewood Cliffs, N.J.: Prentice-Hall.

Shaffir, W. 1974. *Life in a Religious Community.* Montreal: Holt, Rinehart & Winston.

Shapiro, T. 1985. Adolescent language: Its use for diagnosis, group identity, values and treatment. *Adolescent Psychiatry*, 12:297–311.

Shengold, L. and J. McLaughlin. 1976. Panel Report: Changes in psychoanalytic practice and experience. *Int. J. Psychoanal.*, 57:261–274.

Sinha, T. 1965. Psychoanalysis and the family in India. *Bull. Phila. Assn. for Psychoanal.*, 15:114–116.

Solnit, A. 1959. Panel Report: The vicissitudes of ego development in adolescence. *J. Amer. Psa. Assn.*, 7:523–536.

Sorensen, R. 1973. *Adolescent Sexuality in Contemporary America.* New York: World.

Spiro, M. 1987. *Culture and Human Nature: Theoretical Papers.* B. Kilborne and L. Langness, eds. Chicago: University of Chicago Press.

Spitz, E. H. 1988. An insubstantial pageant faded: A psychoanalytic epitaph for New York City subway car graffiti. In H. Risatti, ed., *Postmodern Perspectives: Issues in Contemporary Art*, pp. 260–275. Englewood Cliffs, N.J.: Prentice-Hall, 1990.

# References

Stoller, R., and G. Herdt. 1982. The development of masculinity: A cross-cultural contribution. *J. Amer. Psa. Assn.*, 30:29–59.

Stone, L., and J. Church. 1957. Adolescence as a cultural invention. In A. Esman, ed., *The Psychology of Adolescence*, pp. 7–11. New York: International Universities Press, 1975.

Strober, M., G. Carlson, and J. Green. 1981. Reliability of psychiatric diagnosis in adolescents: Interrater agreement using DSM III. *Arch. Gen. Psychiatry*, 38:141–145.

Symonds, P., and A. Jensen. 1961. *From Adolescent to Adult*. New York: Columbia University Press.

Van Genepp, A. 1908. *The Rites of Passage*. London: Routledge & Kegan Paul, 1960.

Wall, S., and N. Kaltreider. 1977. Changing socio-sexual patterns in gynecological practice. *JAMA*, 237:565–568.

Werner, H. 1948. *Comparative Psychology of Mental Development*. New York: International Universities Press.

Williams, L. 1988. Don't like the new U.S. tone? Zip it, you sleaze. *Int'l. Herald Tribune* (December 19):9.

Williams, T. 1989. *The Cocaine Kids*. Reading, Mass.: Addison-Wesley.

Winokur, G., S. Guze, and A. Pfeiffer. 1959. Developmental and sexual factors in women. *Amer. J. Psychiatry*, 115:1097–1100.

Wright, R. 1945. *Black Boy*. New York: Harper Bros.

Yankelovich, P. 1974. *The New Morality*. New York: McGraw-Hill.

Zamyatin, Y. 1921. *We*. New York: Avon, 1987.

Zinberg, N. 1984. *Drug, Set and Setting*. New Haven: Yale University Press.

# INDEX

# Index

Alcohol, 56–57; and drug abuse, 59

Alpert, Richard, 57

America: rural one-room schoolhouses, 8; social change, 95. *See also* United States

Andrews, A., 5

Anorexia nervosa, 52–53

Anthony, E. J., 32

Antinuclear movement, 89–90

Anxiety, sexual freedom and, 78

Aries, Philippe, 7–9

Aristophanes, 7

Aristotle, 6–7

Arlow, J., 15–16

Athens, ancient, 5–7, 40

Athletes, male, status of, 61

Australia, totemic societies, 13

Autonomy, 32, 39–40; adolescent pregnancy and, 82; preliterate societies and, 13

Baldwin, W., 68

Barglow, P., 25–26

Bar mitzvah, 15–16

Barometer of culture, adolescence as, 94–99

Bas mitzvah, 95

Basquiat, Jean-Michel, 93–94

Baumrind, D., 39

Beaumarchais, Pierre, *Marriage of Figaro*, 8, 42

Beauty, female, 52–53

Behavioral trends, puberty and, 4

Behavior problems, 25. *See also* Deviant behavior; Pathological behavior

Bell, Daniel, 48–49

*Bildungsroman*, 38

Biological factors in adolescence, 4; changes of puberty, 31–32

Bisexuality, attitudes to, 74

*Black Boy*, Wright, 33

Blacks: adolescent pregnancy rate, 80; AIDS information, 79; street gangs, 45

Blos, P., 4, 25, 28

Bourgeoisie, German, 46

Boyer, C. B., 79

Boy Scout movement, 46

Brake, M., 43, 48, 55, 90

Bulimia, 52

Burgess, Anthony, *A Clockwork Orange*, 88

Cameron, M., 69, 76

Capitalism, culture of, 48–49

Career development, female, 77; and adolescent pregnancy, 82

Carlson, G., 27

Case studies: ideological commitment, 89–90; "new sexuality," 70–74

Chandarana, P., 79

Cherubin prototype, 8–9

Chess, S., 69, 76

Child abuse, sexual, 76

Childbearing, contemporary adolescent views, 77

*Childhood and Society*, Erikson, 4

Child labor, Marxist views, 43

Child rearing practices, 94–95

China: Cultural Revolution, 86–88; student uprising, 45–46

Church, J., 16

Civilization: generational conflict and, 28; and sexuality, Freudian views, 15

*Civilization and Its Discontents*, Freud, 14–15

Civil rights, 89

Clarke, J., 47–48

Class structures, England, 47

Clitoral cauterization, 41

*Clockwork Orange, A*, Burgess, 88

Clothing styles, 90

Cocaine, 56

Co-figurative societies, 28

# Index

# Index

# Index

Hispanics: AIDS information, 79; street gangs, 45
History, views of adolescence, 5–17
Hitler Youth, 86–87
Hofferth, S., 68
Hollingshead, A., 43–44; "Elmtown" studies, 37
Homosexuality, 69; AIDS and, 78; in ancient Greece, 7; current attitudes, 74; institutionalized, 40–41
Horne, H., 48
Humanist youth, revolt of, 29
Human nature, 94–95
Hüsen, T., 28

Idealism, 30–31
Identity: sense of, in adolescence, 4, 5; synthetic, of ideology, 86–87
Ideological thinking, 30
Ideology, adolescents and, 86–88
Impotence, "new," 73
Incest, 13, 76; Freudian view, 15
Indian adolescents, 29
Indicators of cultural trends, 94–99
Individual, in capitalist culture, 49
Individuation, 39–40
Industrialized societies, 31, 43, 96, 98; and adolescent behavior, 54; education in, 95; female beauty, 52–53; and youth subculture, 45
Industrial revolution, and adolescence, 9, 16, 39
Infantile omnipotence, fantasies of, 87
Initiation rites, 13–14, 15–17, 40–42
Innovation, cultural, 95
Institutionalization of adolescence, 9, 96

Instruments of change, adolescents as, 86–99
Intellectual development, 30–31, 33
Intergenerational conflict, 25. *See also* Generation gap
Intergenerational continuity, 30, 98
International adolescent culture, 3–4
Intravenous drug use, AIDS and, 78
Ireland: adolescence, 39*n*; adulthood, 40
Israeli adolescents, 56–57

Jackman, B., 43
Jeanne D'Arc, 9
Jefferson, T., 47
Jensen, A., 23
Jewish rites: bar mitzvah, 15–16; bas mitzvah, 95
Jews, American, 95
Johnson, A., 75
Joyce, James, 39; *Portrait of the Artist as a Young Man,* 38
Judeo-Christian tradition, and sexuality, 66
*Jus primae noctis,* 42

Kaltreider, N., 67–68
Kandel, D., 44, 56
Kaplan, L., 9
Keniston, K., 29, 89
Kenyatta, Jomo, 41–42
Kett, J., 11–12
Khan, J., 68
Kinsey, A., 67
Kirby, D., 79
Kirkpatrick, M., 26
Kohlberg, A., 30–31
Kris, E., 10

# Index

Labor force, adolescents in, 16; Marxist views, 43
Lacey, W., 7
Lager louts, 44–45, 48
Language, American, 90–92
Lanson, R., 4
Latency period, Freudian, 14
Latinos: AIDS information, 79; street gangs, 45
Laufer, M., 90
Leary, Timothy, 57
Lesser, G., 44
Leys, S., 87–88
London, adolescent culture, 44–45, 97; seventeenth-century youth gangs, 9, 45
London Sunday Times, 49
Los Angeles, youth subculture, 45
Lower class, behavior patterns, 44
Luepker, R., 54

McAnarney, E., 81
Macauley, Thomas Babington, 9, 45
McLaughlin, J., 76
McRobbie, A., 51
Magical defense efforts, youth subcultures as, 48
Mahler, F., 43
Males: adult status, 40–41; athletes, status of, 61; idealized in teeny-bopper culture, 51–52
—adolescent: ancient Greece, 7; development patterns, 24–25; and "new sexuality," 71–73; and pregnancy, 81
Manners, public, 91
Mao Tse-tung, 86–87
Mari, J. P., 45
Marijuana, 56–58
Marketing strategies of popular music, 50–51
Marriage: age of, in ancient Greece, 7; contemporary adolescent views, 77
Marriage of Figaro, Beaumarchais, 42
Marxist analysis, and youth culture, 43
Masochism, female, 26
Masterson, J., 27
Masturbation, 68; turn-of-the-century views, 38
Maturity, personal, 40
Mead, Margaret, 28, 37, 67; Coming of Age in Samoa, 14–15; and youth culture, 42
Media, and language, 92
Melly, George, 51
Mental health, adolescence and, 24–27
Middle age of parents, teenage children and, 12
Middle Ages, adolescence in, 7–11
Middle-class society, 44; England, 46, 47; gender roles, 95; moralism of, 58–59
—adolescents, 48–49; development patterns, 24; sexual activity, 69, 75
Military training, ancient Greece, 5
Minorities: AIDS information, 79; street gangs, 45
Mitchell, C., 52
Monarca, S., 54
Mönks, F., 29, 33, 39
Mood swings, 25
Morales, E., 79
Moralism: American, 58–59, 81; of adolescence, 30
Morality of sexual freedom, 69–75
Moral judgment, 30–31
Moratorium of choice, 16
Morgan, H., 58
Mother-son incest, 13, 76

# Index

Mozart, Wolfgang Amadeus, *Marriage of Figaro*, 8, 42
Muensterberger, W., 13, 41
Muller, M., 44–45
Murray, D., 45
Music, popular, 50; rock concerts, 92–93

Nandi people, 41, 95
Narcissism: female, 25–26; ideology and, 86
Nazi Germany, Hitler Youth, 86–87
Netherlands, adolescent pregnancy rate, 80
New Guinea, Sambia people, 40–41
"New impotence," 73
"New sexuality," adolescents and, 65–82
New York City, nineteenth-century street gangs, 45
Nineteenth-century: American schools, 11–12; street gangs, 45
Nineteenth-century values, psychoanalysis and, 49
Noncollege youth, and sexual freedom, 69
Non-Western cultures, adolescence in, 12–15
Normative population studies, 23–24

Object relations, in adolescence, 4, 23; female, 25–26
Obscene language, 90–92
Offer, D., 23–24, 26, 28, 66, 76
Offer, J., 23
Oldham, D., 24
Omnipotence, infantile, fantasies of, 87
Openness to change, 98
Orgasm, 73–74

Parents, 28, 44, 98; adolescents and, 29, 32; and sexual behavior of adolescents, 76–77; and socialization of adolescents, 42–43
Passivity, female, 26
Pathological behavior, 22–23, 26–27
Peer groups, 14, 42, 44; and development, 24; socialization by, 28
Peplau, L., 68
Performance, sexual, and new freedom, 73–74
Performers, pop stars, 50–51
Personality, formation of, 95
Perverse sexual behavior, 75–76
Pfeiffer, A., 67
Piaget, J., 30–31
Pirie, P., 54
Plains Indians, rites of passage, 13
Plato, 5
*Playboy of the Western World, The*, Synge, 40
Politeness, deterioration of, 91
Politics, radical, influences, 29
Pop idols, 50–51
Popular music, 50–51, 92–93
Pornography, and sexual behavior, 75–76
*Portrait of the Artist as a Young Man*, Joyce, 38
Post-figurative societies, 28
Postindustrial societies, 96
Post-World War II youth cultures, England, 46–48
Poverty, culture of, 81
Powerlessness of youth, 55
Pregnancy, adolescents, 80–82
Preliterate cultures: adolescence in, 12–15, 16; adult status, 40
Premarital relationships, 69, 77
Primitive societies, 17, 94–95
Promiscuity, 75, 79; homosexual, 78

# Index

Propositional thinking, 30–31
Pseudoheterosexuality, female phase, 25
Psychoactive drugs, 57
Psychoanalysis: future of, 99; nineteenth-century values, 49
Psychoanalytic views of adolescence, 4, 21–23, 28–31, 39, 98–99; female, 25–26
Psychopathological behavior, 22–23, 26–27
Psychosocial model of adolescence, 4
Puberty, 17, 31–32, 97–98; psychoanalytic view, 4; sexual component, 12–13
Pumereiga, A., 52
Punk clothing, 90

Racism, 61
Radical politics, 29
Rakoff, V., 53
Rape, 60–61
Red Guard, China, 86–88
Reeves, J., 13, 43
Religion, and sexuality, 74–75
Religious groups, and sex education, 81
Reminiscences, fictionalized, 38
Revolution: sexual, 65–66; social, youth movements, 86
Rhodes, Zandra, 90
Rites of passage, 13–15, 17; and cultural change, 15–16; female, 41–42
Roberts, B., 47
Rock culture, 92–93; traditional double standard, 52
Roles: expectations in adolescence, 4; female, teeny-bopper culture, 51–52
*Romeo and Juliet,* Shakespeare, 10, 45

Rousseau, Jean-Jacques, *Emile,* 9
Rural families, changes, 96
Rushdie, S., *The Satanic Verses,* 96–97

Sambia people, New Guinea, 40–41
San Francisco, AIDS education, 79
*Satanic Verses, The,* Rushdie, 96–97
Schaefer, M., 25–26
Schmidt, G., 68
Schools, 43; medieval, 8; nineteenth-century America, 11–12. *See also* Education
Sebald, H., 9, 40, 45
*Secret of Suzanne, The,* Wolf-Ferrari, 54
Self-esteem: culture and, 47–48; and sexual performance, 73; masturbation and, 38–39
Self-realization, female, 77
Serial monogamy, 67–68, 70, 77
Seventeenth century: schools, 8, 11; youth gangs, 9, 45
Sex education: and AIDS, 79; and adolescents behavior, 82; objections to, 81
Sexual abuse, 60–61; of children, 76
Sexuality, adolescent, 12–15; culture and, 40, 65–82; Freudian views, 14
Sexual mores, changes in, 65
Shaffir, W., 16
Shakespeare, William, *Hamlet,* 10; *Henry IV,* 10–11; *Romeo and Juliet,* 45; *Winter's Tale,* 9–10
Shamans, 16n
Shame: contraceptive use and, 81; sexual activity and, 66–67
Shapiro, T., 73, 99
Shengold, L., 76

# Index

Sigusch, V., 68
Single-parent families, and adolescent pregnancy, 81
Sinha, T., 29, 96
Sixteenth century, schools, 8
Skinheads, 44–45, 48
Smoking, 53–54
Smuggling of marijuana, 58
Social adolescence, 13–15; end of, 40
Social change, 33; adolescents and, 85–99
Social dependency, and adolescent pregnancy, 82
Socialization, 17, 42–43; by peer groups, 28; television and, 50
Social justice, ideas of, 31
Social relationships of adolescence, 32
Social support, and adolescent pregnancy, 81
Socioeconomic tendencies, and adolescent behavior, 54
Sociological view of adolescence, 4, 37–42, 45–46
Solnit, A., 23
Sorensen, R., 67–68, 72, 76–77
Soviet Komsomol, 86
Sparta, adolescents in, 5
Speech, uninhibited, 91–92
Spiro, Melford, 94–95
Spitz, E. H., 93
Stoller, R., 40
Stone, L., 16
Strachey, J., 14–15
Street gangs, 45
Strober, M., 27
Student disturbances, 28–29, 88–89; in developing nations, 45
Study of adolescence, 99
Subcultures, adolescent, 44
Substance abuse, crosscultural differences, 56–57. See also Drug culture

Subway graffiti, 93–94
Success, and sexual maturation, 67
Surgent adolescent development, male, 24
Symonds, P., 23
Synchronic perspectives, 37
Synge, John Millington, *The Playboy of the Western World*, 40

Teachers, views of, 43
Teddy boys, 48
Teeny-boppers, 51
Television, 49–50; and violence, 60
Ten Houten, W., 13, 43
Thinness, female, 52–53
Third-world adolescents, 45
Thomas A., 69, 76
*Three Essays*, Freud, 15
Three Mile Island incident, 89–90
Tobacco use, 53–54
Totalitarian regimes, 86–87
Totemic societies, rites of passage, 13
Traditional societies, adult status, 40
Traditions, 95
Tumultuous growth, adolescent development, 25
Turmoil of adolescence, 21–27
Twentieth century, youth cultures, 46–48
Two-parent families, 42

United States: civil rights, 89; cultural values, 55; middle-class moralism, 58–59
—adolescents, 11–12; parental influence, 44; pregnancy rate, 80–81; sexual activity, 68–69; substance abuse, 56–57
Urbanization, adolescence and, 45, 96

# Index

Valli, E., 43
Values: of adolescent drug users,
59–60; in American culture, 55;
sexual, 60–61, 67; twentieth-
century capitalist, 49
Van Genepp, A., 13
Vietnam War, 89; protestors, 91
Violence, culture and, 61
Violent language, 90–92

Wall, S., 67–68
Wandervögel, 46
Warrior tribes, rites of passage, 13
Werner, Heinz, 17, 94
West Side Story, 10
Williams, L., 90–91
Williams, T., 59–60
Winokur, G., 67

Winter's Tale, Shakespeare, The,
9–10
Wolf-Ferrari, Ermanno, The Secret
of Suzanne, 54
Women's movement, 91–92; ado-
lescent development studies, 25
Work, and self-esteem, 47–48
Working-class adolescents: in Eng-
land, 46–48; sexual freedom, 75
Working mothers, 42
Wright, Richard, Black Boy, 33

Yankelovich, D., 69
Youth culture, 42–55; ancient
Greece, 7

Zinberg, N., 58